"Now and again, a book comes along that, as you turn each page, feels like you're involved in a rich, heartfelt conversation between two old friends. This is one of those books: incredibly readable, instantly relatable and threaded throughout with wisdom and insight. At a time when the early education sector is struggling to put childhood and positive relationship at its centre, each chapter contains the reassurance and the 'story' of why we need humanness in our practice more than ever.

I found myself nodding along with Jamel and Sonia time and again as they conversed – they have created a truly heartwarming, indeed soulwarming, Early Years book – you will be an even better practitioner with its companionship."

Greg Bottrill, *author and childhood advocate*

"This book deftly unpicks the intricacies of building positive relationships in early years practice through each author's own experiences of supporting children, families, colleagues and the wider community. Sonia and Jamel's life histories within the profession provide a valuable contrast and illustrate the diversity of childhood practice. Yet, they also draw attention to a number of fundamentals in creating a sense of belonging, safety and security with young children and their families. This book further provides a novel reflection on the multiple pathways that can lead to a career in the early years, including both the joyous moments and the challenges of such a journey. Overall, it is a text that will appeal to all those in the profession who are drawn to furthering

T0003347

their knowledge and understanding of positive relationships in practice."

"This unique union of minds brings much needed perspectives into our sector. A stark reminder that, no matter what knowledge and experiences that we bring to our role, we are all dedicated to placing children at the heart of our practice. The authors capture the essence of the adult-child relationship, describing everyday connections that spark emotion in children and adults. This book provides detailed examples of interactions that may seem unremarkable to those outside of the sector, but they are a fascinating insight into the very important role that adults play in families' lives. A glaring reminder of the need for a valued and varied workforce. This book helps us to consider wider issues that affect the communities that we serve and our role as early years educators within that. This book reminded me of my 'why'. Why we do what we do."

Building Positive Relationships in the Early Years

In this unique and original book, Jamel Carly Campbell and Sonia Mainstone-Cotton come together to have an open and honest conversation about developing positive and responsive relationships in the early years.

The book is divided into three main chapters – building positive relationships with children; with other professionals; and with families and the wider community – and each conversation explores a range of key themes, from building trust and listening to the voice of the child, to diversifying practice and creating a setting that represents the wider community. These discussions encourage the reader to consider the connections we make every day, to rethink and empower their practice, and to place a much higher value on their position as an early years advocate.

With reflective questions included to allow the reader to think about their own practice, as well as suggested further reading to explore the themes in more depth, this engaging and accessible book is a must-read for all early years professionals – and, importantly, encourages every practitioner to begin new conversations of their own.

Jamel Carly Campbell is an early years educator, early years consultant and aspiring children's author. Early years is his speciality, and he has been in the industry for over 20 years. He has also worked in youth clubs and schools, and mentored children with SEND. Jamel is one of the UK's Men in the Early Years ambassadors and has featured on CBeebies "Tiny happy people" as an Early Years advisor.

Sonia Mainstone-Cotton is a freelance nurture consultant. She currently works in a specialist team supporting 3- and 4-year-olds who have social, emotional and mental health needs. She also trains staff across the country, working with children's centres, schools, nurseries, charities and churches. Sonia has written eight books.

Little Minds Matter:

Promoting Social and Emotional Wellbeing in the Early Years

Series Advisor: Sonia Mainstone-Cotton

The *Little Minds Matter* series promotes best practice for integrating social and emotional health and wellbeing into the early years setting. It introduces practitioners to a wealth of activities and resources to support them in each key area: from providing access to ideas for unstructured, imaginative outdoor play; activities to create a sense of belonging and form positive identities; and, importantly, strategies to encourage early years professionals to create a workplace that positively contributes to their own wellbeing, as well as the quality of their provision. The *Little Minds Matter* series ensures that practitioners have the tools they need to support every child.

Outdoor Play for Healthy Little Minds
Practical Ideas to Promote Children's Wellbeing in the Early Years
Sarah Watkins

Supporting the Wellbeing of Children with SEND
Essential Ideas for Early Years Educators
Kerry Payne

Supporting Behaviour and Emotions in the Early Years
Strategies and Ideas for Early Years Educators
Tamsin Grimmer

A Guide to Mental Health for Early Years Educators
Putting Wellbeing at the Heart of Your Philosophy and Practice
Kate Moxley

Supporting the Wellbeing of Children with EAL
Essential Ideas for Practice and Reflection
Liam Murphy

Building Positive Relationships in the Early Years
Conversations to Empower Children, Professionals,
Families and Communities
Jamel Carly Campbell and Sonia Mainstone-Cotton

Building Positive Relationships in the Early Years

Conversations to Empower Children, Professionals, Families and Communities

Jamel Carly Campbell and
Sonia Mainstone-Cotton

Routledge
Taylor & Francis Group

LONDON AND NEW YORK

Cover image: Raul Hillers, aged 4, enjoys drawing pictures using different forms of media and mark making implements. He gifts his masterpieces to his peers, family and teachers

First published 2023
by Routledge
4 Park Square, Milton Park, Abingdon, Oxon OX14 4RN

and by Routledge
605 Third Avenue, New York, NY 10158

Routledge is an imprint of the Taylor & Francis Group, an informa business

British Library Cataloguing-in-Publication Data
A catalogue record for this book is available from the British Library

Library of Congress Cataloging-in-Publication Data
A catalog record has been requested for this book

ISBN: 978-1-032-06248-8 (hbk)
ISBN: 978-1-032-06246-4 (pbk)
ISBN: 978-1-003-20137-3 (ebk)

DOI: 10.4324/9781003201373

Typeset in Optima
by Deanta Global Publishing Services, Chennai, India

Contents

Foreword

The foreword for this book in the Little Minds Matters series is slightly different from the others. Firstly, I co-authored the book with Jamel. For those who have read other books in this series, you will notice this one has a different feel to it. This book is based on three conversations recorded between Jamel and myself about building positive relationships in the early years. Each chapter has a separate focus based around exploring pedagogical practice. We both come from very different backgrounds and experiences: Jamel is in his 30s, he is a black male Londoner; I am a white, almost-50-year-old, West Country woman.

In this book, we explore and discuss many varied subjects about the early years and our experience of working in it. The topics range from working with families, working in multi-disciplinary teams, how to increase diversity in the workplace, children and adults' wellbeing, representation and inclusion. The intention was to cover different topics within each focal area, but you will see that certain subjects get mentioned in each chapter, as there are inevitably some overlaps.

I hope we have managed to capture some of the delight and enthusiasm we had in our conversations. We discovered we share a love for the work we do; yes, we have very different experiences, but we also discovered many connections and similarities. I learnt masses from talking with Jamel. He is such a caring, sensitive and hugely knowledgeable man, it was an absolute delight to share these conversations with him.

I hope this book will give you some space to reflect on your practice. If you have the chance, I encourage you to find someone in the early years community to have a conversation with about your differing practice. We can learn so much when we listen to one another's experiences.

Sonia Mainstone-Cotton
Series Advisor
January 2021

Introduction

Sonia has worked in early years since she was 16 (she will be 50 on her next birthday). She is a freelance nurture consultant, currently working in a specialist team in Bath, supporting 3- and 4-year-olds who have social, emotional and mental health needs. She also trains staff across the country on the wellbeing of both children and staff. Sonia has written eight books, mostly focusing on children and staff wellbeing. She enjoys wild swimming all year round, all over the country, to support her own wellbeing.

Jamel C is an early years educator, early years consultant and children's author in his 30s. He has been in the industry for over 20 years. Early years is his speciality, but he has worked in youth clubs and schools, and mentored and supported children with special educational needs and disabilities (SEND). Jamel is one of the UK's Men in the Early Years champions/ambassadors. He is passionate about the early years and stresses the importance of having men in the early years, and the importance of having a balanced, diverse and inclusive workforce, curriculum and pedagogy.

The foundation to our pedagogy is centred around the four themes of the early years foundation stage, positive relationships being one of those themes. Personal social and emotional

DOI: 10.4324/9781003201373-1

development (PSED) is a crucial skill; it is important that children have a strong foundation of personal, relational skills, but often they don't have the opportunity to fully develop these – and it's incredibly important to create opportunities, *from the foundation stage of their lives*, so that they can understand and develop successful relationships in the future.

Facial recognition and the developing understanding of facial expressions have been hindered by the constant need to shield our faces with visors and masks during the pandemic. In this time, we have seen how important current technology is, but also, on the other hand, the concerns it has raised due to children becoming used to a different and instant means of communication. A breakdown of face-to-face interactions can make real-time social engagement challenging.

This book looks at positive relationships holistically, picking apart different types of connections, bonds and interactions between our children, their families, their parents/carers, and our colleagues and staff teams, acknowledging their intersecting nature and their impact on wellbeing and learning.

The book takes a unique and original approach as we – an inner-city black man from Lewisham and a white woman from Bath and Somerset – have each taken different journeys in the profession and bring our own insights on a range of themes, from creating a culture of belonging in your setting, to working as part of a truly multi-disciplinary team. Although we share both similarities and differences in perspectives, during our conversations we hope to demonstrate the importance of placing the child at the centre of all early years work.

There is a need in the sector to hear a range of voices and experiences, and other practitioners shouldn't be afraid to share their own thoughts. The conversations in this book take a free-flowing nature but touch upon key areas and themes, all of which are pertinent to early years practitioners and some of which might be areas of worry or concern. In the conversations, we share fundamentals of our practices and also include points of reflection for the reader and recommendations of where to go for further information on important topics.

We know you will enjoy.

Best,
Jamel and Sonia

Building positive relationships with children in your care

In this chapter, Sonia and Jamel will be discussing:

- The central importance of interactions, connections and forming positive relationships
- Belonging, trust, and feeling safe and secure
- Representation and inclusion
- Supporting children with SEMH and the value of the practitioner–child relationship
- How to encourage children to have positive relationships with each other
- How to create a setting that represents the wider community
- Building bonds and an understanding that the class is a community, whether neurodiverse or neurotypical

Building positive relationships with children

Jamel   Building positive relationships with children in your care. So how do we go about doing so?

DOI: 10.4324/9781003201373-2

Sonia   The key is building trust with a child and keeping that in mind at the beginning of any relationship. We want the child to know that we're an adult who really believes in them. Thinking about that moment when a child walks in the door, or you walk in a door, and how you present yourself, how you look at them, how you smile. When I arrive in a school, I want a child to clock me and go, Yes, it's Sonia. She thinks I'm great.

Jamel   Yeah, when you walk into a room and you see a child just elated, elated like, "wow, this person looks like someone I want to talk to, their body language, their aura, their vibe". It's interesting and amazing how children are so receptive of your vibe and of your aura, and straightaway they're interested in who you are, where you come from, and your interests.

Sonia   Definitely, but in the same way, I've observed children seeing certain people and totally ignoring them. The message the child is giving is "I'm not talking to you" because they know the person isn't really interested in them. The contrast is when they know the person likes them and wants to spend time with them. I've got a little boy that I work with at the moment, as I walk into the classroom as soon as he sees me, it doesn't matter what they're doing, he will shriek with delight, shouting "Sonia's here". He darts across the classroom, flings himself at me and says, "I missed you so much". It's just delightful, it's just wonderful. Such a great way to be welcomed – he feels loved by me and I feel loved by him.

Jamel   It's important for us to understand that not all children are going to react to us like that and it's about giving them time. There was a little boy in one of my groups that I've worked with that was very wary of me, and when I spoke he would shudder because my voice is so deep. I just gave him time, I didn't force the interaction. I would say hello to encourage him. Then, one day, he just walked up to me and gave me a car. Then one day I had a dinosaur, and I gave him the dinosaur. The next time I was there, I gave him another toy, and then he spoke to me and then asked me about my gold tooth. When I saw his parents, I'd say hello to demonstrate that I'm a cool dude, it's okay to talk to me, and we have taken steps to build up that relationship. It has to be authentic – organic and not forced.

Sonia   Totally. Children know when it isn't authentic, they can see through it. It's important that we know and respect our different children. I've got another little boy who, at the beginning of the school year, was selected mute and we just couldn't get anything from him. And that was fine, that was okay. So actually, I think for about two months, my sessions with him involved no words from him, and that was absolutely fine. There was no pressure. Whereas now, he will chat, which is amazing, but it was about giving him space and for him to know that's okay – if you don't want to talk, that's fine.

Jamel   Yeah. And through that process, you're then forming a connection. You're building a connection with that child so they can look at you and say, "Sonia understands me, Jamel understands me, the practitioner understands me". And I've seen it where there's been a child that is selective mute or even preverbal, and just taking time and leaving them to interact with you on their own basis and in their own way. And sometimes that interaction could come from an activity, that interaction can come from you doing something random like singing a song or role playing, or just taking an interest in what that child likes. I always stress the fact that the child-centred approach is paramount to practice, understanding that each child is unique and understanding their uniqueness, understanding who they are, helps that interaction and helps to build up that level of trust.

Sonia   Absolutely, and I think it's going that extra mile to really find out what it is that works for them, what it is that they're interested in. I'm always saying this to staff – find out what that child's interest is, then you can use that to really connect with them, and they feel so great when that's been recognised in them. When you suddenly start talking about the dinosaurs, when they're fascinated with dinosaurs, My Little Pony, or whatever it is, it doesn't matter. When you connect in that way, they feel like they've been heard, they have that sense of, somebody's noticed me and values me for who I am right now. Yeah, I think that's so powerful. We know that as adults don't we. When you asked me, how's your swimming going Sonia, I felt like, yeah, he's remembered that, he's valued how that's really important. And it's exactly the same with children. That connection is so important.

Jamel Most definitely. Those key features of who they are, what makes them *them*. And it gives you a level of joint interest. For instance, when I'm with my groups, I would always watch the children's cartoons and get into it, be it Paw Patrol or Octonauts, all these different programmes. And the children, they will look at me in amazement because I watched their programmes and know about the different characters and so on, and they will hold conversations about different things they have seen, and there's a fluid, organic exchange based on the effort that you've made to find out what their interests are. It's not about just knowing the name of the programme. Do you know the characters and features? Because characters are really important to our children because they connect the characters to themselves.

Sonia It shows you've just gone that extra mile and made extra effort to go and find out. I had one little boy, he was wary for a while, and I was really struggling to figure out what his interests were and what made him click, and then I discovered it was wild animals and owls. Owls, particularly, and birds of prey, he just adored them. So, with that information I knew what I was going to do: I found out about birds of prey, and I did a little bit of research and was then able to have those conversations with him, and he suddenly just blossomed, you could see the light and the glint in his eyes. And that's what I love – when you can see a glint in a child's eye that illustrates you've connected in some way, you've got somewhere with them, which is powerful. It's that sense of, I belong here. Somebody really knows something about me and what I like. I think that links with a sense of belonging, the question of what does it mean to belong in a place. I think it's an interesting question and one we often ask in our work – how do we know when a child feels like they belong? It's an interesting question to ask staff – what does that look like for our children?

Jamel   And you've heard me speak about this before, about the fact that children need to feel connected to the setting, there needs to be a range of things for them to do that they like and enjoy, and like always. I'm just one of those people where, when I'm in a setting, I would look at a child whose interest could be puzzles and I will make sure that that child has access to at least five or six puzzles, and even, even when the child is coming into the setting, the initial drop off, I'll be like, "oh guess what we've got out today, we're going to take out puzzles, if you want you can select what puzzles you want"; empowering them and showing them that what they like is available for them. And then, when the child goes home and has conversations with their family members or whoever, they'll say, "guess what I did today!?", they will talk about how we have big puzzles, small puzzles, and hold a positive conversation about their interest, connecting their interest to the setting. This helps the child to associate the setting with fun and freedom. The child will see the setting as a place where they can do what they enjoy. A child may like art – it's for us to then elaborate on that, maybe taking children out to different trips, putting things in the environment that they enjoy, like drawing, free mark making, access to paints, free access to whatever they like so they can really explore that and extend their learning experience. I love it because then you see the child thrive, you see that interest develop – they start off on a stage of just making marks, then it's recognisable marks, then they begin describing the marks and telling us what they're drawing and explaining what these different objects are, "these are circles", "these are squares" and "these lines, zigzags, are lightning" and so on. The children develop a feeling, a sense of pride when these marks are then presented or displayed within the environment, that sense of achievement.

Building positive relationships with families

Sonia   I think that's interesting. We have that relationship with the children and, in some ways, that's the easy bit because we're with them regularly. But then how do you build that relationship with the child's family, with their carers? I don't know about you but there are certainly some families that I work with, actually quite a lot of families that I work with, where they are so wary of professionals. They may not have had a great experience of school themselves; they might be quite anxious and have poor mental health. They may be worried about their child starting school; they might be wary and untrusting. Some of the children I work with can be quite violent, the parents are often really worried that they're going to be excluded. That is a lot for parents to be thinking about. I work hard at the beginning of the year, with parents, to help them know that I'm here to love their child, I'm here to advocate for their child, to really get to know them. One of the things I say to parents is, "tell me something about your child that just brings you joy". And that's just such a lovely way of helping parents to go, oh she really does want to know something good about my child, she doesn't just want to know that he bites and kicks and runs off and these are his triggers. That question can help to break down some of the barriers. A question to ask ourselves is, "how do we help parents to know they can trust us?"

Jamel   I think that sometimes with some parents there is that "us versus them" kind of way of seeing things, and they constantly think that they're under the microscope – that practitioners are judging their parenting, when really we're here to support, and the parent partnership is what helps that consistency in their child's development. And I tell a lot of the practitioners and professionals that I work with that. It's important to build up those bonds, it's important to reassure our parents, and it's important to understand that parents aren't always going to understand us and where we're coming from, and they don't understand our jargon as well. That's another thing. So, we need to make ourselves available for them and hold those conversations with parents in a way that they can digest, be it a pedagogical conversation or be it just a general conversation about how their day is going: "How are you today, Mum?", "how are you today, Dad?", "how are you today, Carer?" It's important that we ask these things and check in on them so they know that we actually care.

Sonia   Yeah, definitely. And I think, also, when we're able to say something really positive, you can see that recognition of "oh you've really noticed". Similar to the way a child feels like they've been noticed, it's also helpful for parents to know you have noticed their child. I was able to say to a dad recently how his boys had been able to name all the bugs when we went on a bug hunt, I told him that other children I had worked with didn't have the bug names. I told him how thrilled I was to hear his boys naming the bugs and recognised that he must have taught them. He was just beaming. He was so happy to hear that and to have that positive feedback on his children, it was just a small thing but it really boosted him, which was great.

Jamel   And, in turn, parents would then hold dialogue with their children about what they've done in nursery or their setting that further helps to build the child's perspective of who the practitioner is and helps to build up that level of trust. So if, therefore, if they can see a good relationship between parent and practitioner, then that helps them to build up their perception and the trust with us. And another thing it makes me think about is transitions and how good parent and practitioner relationships help children with the transition, because that initial phase is like coming from a home environment to being in a setting. It is such a big difference, from the food, even the smells, and aesthetically it is different.

Sonia Absolutely, that's why I'm such an advocate of home visits. It's been interesting this year as none of the children I work with had a home visit before they started school. Because of COVID the schools decided they couldn't do it. Lots of staff have recognised we need to get back to doing them. They enable us to see the child in a different environment. The home environment is so different to school or nursery. Home visits also enable you, in a much more informal way, to have conversations with parents. There's also something good about you as a professional, not being in your environment. When you do a home visit and a family lets you into their home, that's a massive privilege, it really is, the whole being offered a cup of tea or a drink and all of those sorts of things. I think we can sometimes take it for granted but it's a massive privilege. Sitting in somebody's home, and they've allowed you in it, it's different to you having them come into your classroom. Also being able to see the child in their own home, when you later see them in your setting you can ask them if they remember when they showed you their cat or when you played with their Lego together, the children love that. Yeah, home visits, I think, are really powerful.

Jamel Most definitely. Children act differently at home to the way they will act in a setting as well. And it gives you a deeper understanding of who the child is when you see them around their toys, their sofa, their room, their family and so on. And you can see it even with eating and things like that. Some parents will say "Oh, he or she doesn't eat this at home", but then in the setting they will. Or they don't climb at home, but in the setting they do, and so on, so you have this mash-up of behaviours. And it's good to have that information to reference when you're in the setting. Also, I think with home visits, you definitely can understand the structure of a family from a cultural perspective, even from an economic and financial perspective as well. And then you're able to give support. What I used to do with some of my parents who couldn't afford mark making tools, Crayons, paper, paint brushes, I used to give it to them because, a lot of the time, we've got these budgets in schools and a lot of our resources at the end of the year were getting thrown away. So, I would be like, "Here, take this". And that sense of helping also helps to form a relationship, like "this teacher, this practitioner, really cares". And from that, you're then further helping the child to develop and have consistency. I found through this pandemic, and through the lockdown, the importance of understanding home dynamics has come to light and to the centre of everything we've been doing, especially with these zoom sessions and people having to turn their home environment into a learning environment.

Sonia   I think as early years practitioners we often need to have a very good emotional antenna. In past jobs I have worked in family support work. There would be times when I would walk into a home and it would feel like a loving and safe environment. But the counter is also true. At other times I have walked into a home and thought there's an atmosphere here right now, I can't put my finger on it, but something isn't right. Recognising and noticing these things can be so important – when the child is in your setting and they're a bit edgy, you can wonder if everything is okay in the home and remember the feeling you had. From this you might have further conversations with your colleagues and the family, maybe also with other professionals.

Jamel   Yeah. And, from that perspective, you then understand the importance of the class as its own little community, as its own little place, its own sanctum, if we call it that, because sometimes, for a lot of children, school is an escape from the turbulence of the household. Some children, they really look forward to coming into school and having Zoom sessions. While home schooling you see some of the children will request to see other children and really get upset if they don't see their friends. And when school opened again, they would hug each other and play. They were so glad to see each other. I remember a child saw me from the windows, J, waving at me and so excited and he just felt that sense of belonging and that sense of love. You feel a little twinkle in your heart. So yeah, having that sense of community and a sense of connection is so important. And having the teacher as a go-to and your friends as a go-to, as well.

A feeling of belonging

Sonia   That doesn't just happen, that takes a lot of work. You can really tell when you walk into a school or a nursery group and it feels like a family. You know that the staff have worked really hard. It's not just accidental. It's an intentional decision of the leadership: we are going to nurture this group. So together, we care for one another. We nurture one another. We look out for one another. It is really noticeable when we see that in staff teams. I can think of a few staff teams where they really look after one another. And what is also noticeable is how that then ripples to the children too.

Jamel   And it's being in your practice and being purposeful in your approach. I feel like the things that we do daily as practitioners, as teachers, and so forth, really helps to build up the self-esteem and the resilience, the wellbeing of our children – just being available, being there. Taking an interest in their day, taking an interest in what's going on with them and holding a little conversation, even with babies when you're working with babies. Interacting, saying hello and taking five minutes out of your time to really connect, to give them the eye contact, and so on, really helps their development cognitively and emotionally. And you can see, as you interact continually, that they respond to you more and more and then they become more comfortable with you being there, to the point where they might even reach out to you and want you to pick them up and cuddle them and so on.

For those authentic interactions, those purposeful interactions, children, as we said before, pick up on your vibe. They read a lot from your expressions when you're sad and do different things that illustrate that they understand how you're feeling. I've had an instance where I was a little sad and a bit worn and a child just came up to me and hugged my leg and looked up at me and said, "You okay, JJ?" I was like, how do you know I'm feeling like this? And I just said thank you and gave them a hug, and it made me realise that children are always watching. We need to be aware of ourselves, we need to be aware of how we express ourselves, and just be aware of how we're feeling and understand that if we're feeling angry, it's okay to be angry, sad, frustrated, but understand that to our little people we are role models. And they learn so much from us via the interactions that we have with each other. Be it the interactions that we have with the parents or the interactions that we have with other children. They are calculating a perspective of us.

Sonia   They really are, and you can notice that actually if you have a member of staff who finds a particular child tricky. It's really interesting to see how the other children respond to that child. I've had a child recently where they were blamed for everything. Now, admittedly, there were some things that happened, but he really wasn't behind everything and the staff were quick to jump to the presumption it was him. They began to realise that if there was a problem this little boy would be blamed for things, and he wasn't even in the nursery. When I was unpicking that with staff it took a lot for them to go, actually, yeah maybe that was our attitude too. You have to be really self-reflective, don't you, and so careful because, actually, that's the other issue – children can hear and start copying.

Jamel   Yeah, even things like the way that we interact with our environments, like sitting on tables, for instance, children will copy that behaviour. It might even be the fact that we say good morning, hello, thank you, please – our manners – children pick up on that. And I think that whole being conscious, being present attitude helps to form positive attitudes.

I think also just understanding the culture and the flow of the nursery as a community, and the concept of the wider community, is important. And I just want to say that to bring it into the whole inclusive practice side of things, because sometimes there was miscommunication because we didn't understand the dynamics of our families – their backgrounds and their traditions.

Sonia   I agree. I think it's giving people permission to say I don't know about this, can you tell me? When I first started, I worked with young children who had feeding difficulties and I worked with families in their homes. Early in my job I worked with an Asian family and for their mealtimes they sat on the floor together around a small table and would eat mostly with their hands. An important part of the job was that I needed to sit and eat with the family. With this family I asked them to tell me about their mealtimes and traditions because I wanted to join in with them and respect their way of doing mealtimes. It was great, the mother said it would be easier if I ate what they were eating and asked if I was happy to share their food. I was delighted to have that opportunity, to learn from them, and I had a wonderful time sharing their meals with them. It taught me early on in my career that it's okay to say "I don't know, please can I learn?"

Jamel Yeah, it is, and asking those vital questions is so important in terms of the way that you can transfer the home environment into the setting. Maybe it's through your menus, maybe it's having different objects within the room that connect to home, be it pots, plates, dolls, books and so on. Children need to see something that comes from home. And music as well. A lot of the time in settings, we're so scared to play music. It's not about Nursery Rhymes, it's not Twinkle, Twinkle Little Star. Play some music, play some reggae – and these things can be done outside of cultural events. Why does it have to be during cultural months that we're celebrating these different communities and the things that they do? I think that as practitioners a lot of our sector has got into this whole box ticking way, this tick box practice, and it says in one of our documents that the framework is not a tick box process, it is about understanding the child. It's about understanding that pedagogy is centred on who the child is as an individual and combining that with your approach to teaching. And then dipping your subject knowledge in there as well and having that holistic approach, basically. It's about understanding that this is a child – this is who they are, this is their background, and celebrating it. And this is how we can use it to extend their learning.

Sonia   As you say, it's about embedding practice, not just having a week to do cultural awareness but really embedding it into our everyday practice. My heart sinks when I see special weeks, it so often feels token-istic. We need to embed cultural awareness into our everyday practice. We can all find out where the children are from, the different cultures that they're from, and celebrate that regularly. It doesn't matter if you don't know – go find out. Ask the children and families, bring the parents in, involve them and engage with them. But please, don't just do it as a one-off week once a year.

Jamel   Be creative, put some effort in and care. If you're doing a maths activity, you can get Russian dolls and line them up and so on. There are so many different things that you can do, and that helps to connect home to the setting. And I think that's so important. This is a place of care. This is a place where children are spending the majority of their time and they need to feel that sense of home.

Sonia   We have talked about the importance of understanding the cultures our children experience and for us to understand how families live. Of course, this is relevant for all children and we need to recognise the broad range of different cultures. I live in a rural, small village. In the village primary school that my children went to a lot of the children had parents who were either farmers or hunters. We had children who quite regularly talked about how their dad shot hares or rabbits, we would regularly have parents giving away pheasants and rabbits in the playground at the end of the school day. The children would talk about guns in the context of catching food for tea. In that context, for some of the children it was a normal part of country living, but of course, in an urban context, a conversation about guns could be very different and cause huge concerns. It's important we understand our families, and for us to know what's going on in that community and what they do. I had one little boy who was from a farming family. At the age of four he told me he was a farmer and he had his own hens he looked after. This little boy hated maths and numbers and said he couldn't do it. However, if you gave him cows to count, that was no problem at all. If you told him you needed to know how many cows needed milking, he would happily count the cows. But if you gave him blocks to count, he wouldn't engage.

Jamel   Yeah, yeah, because it's based on what his day-to-day life is and what he sees. It's just understanding, understanding who that child is and where they come from – a lot of learning. In some children's backgrounds, as you said, they are farmers and hunters and so on, they spend a lot of time outside and it's important to understand that. And, in my practice, what I'll do is I'll do activities outside because that child is used to it – maybe they don't like being cooped up and they need space to run, space to climb, space to explore, and in some ways, you are blocking the child's learning if you don't understand that. If you don't understand that there's a particular way that child likes to learn, a particular way that child likes to play during their time at home. This is how they pass time. They're woken up by the sounds of a cockerel, they go out and feed the pigs, feed the chickens and so on.

And I can actually relate that back to life in the Caribbean. We're woken up by chickens and we're taken by grandparents, uncles, aunts, it's your responsibility to feed all the animals, to bring the goats down and so on. You're taught that from a young age, and you had to do that before going into school. You spend a lot of time outside. Some of the classes are even done outside, where they've got like blackboards outside and so on and they will teach the children, so the majority of time is spent outdoors even though there's a school building. It is very open plan, free flowing and there's a lot going on, even the sounds. And I've noticed, bringing it back to England, the school environment in rural areas is totally different to the school environment in the inner cities. I worked in a school in Reading a long time ago and they had a big open playground, they had their own forest school section, they had chickens and they had free flow. But in the inner cities they don't have the space to do that free flow and for children to have that access. So, imagine a child coming from that environment, then moving into the inner city and not having that space to run around. That can build frustration, and a lot of the time the focus will then become on that child's behaviour, but not on the antecedent of that behaviour, which is the dynamic that they came from.

Sonia   And it's always recognising, isn't it, what's that behaviour communicating? That's my mantra all the time – this child is telling us something here. We may not necessarily fully understand what they're telling us, but our job is to figure out what it is that they're trying to communicate.

Jamel   Definitely, then to build on their experiences and show them that even though the environment is laid out the way it is, this is what I'm going to do to adapt my environment to support your needs. And another thing that I think is really key is understanding the importance of our children building relationships with each other. Understanding that that their individual characteristics are important and making them celebrate each other. Because children will hold conversations about difference freely. "Little Jamel is brown, but I am pink", and so on. Or "Jamel's daddy's got long black hair, my hair is brown". There's a little girl that I've worked with and she's just got this prime attachment to this black doll. She loves it. She's like, inseparable, they're inseparable. Children appreciate difference and she loves that doll because the doll is different. That doll looks like one of her friends. It's important that we understand this, and we celebrate this – we celebrate that difference, because in some places there is no diversity. But one thing that will happen to a vast majority is when they go out into the world, the wider community, they will have to experience diversity and it will be a big shock for them, so it's important for us, as the practitioner, to ensure that children are having these experiences, and that knowledge – that difference – should be celebrated.

Sonia Totally, and in our area, it is a really big issue because I live in an area that's predominantly white. Somerset is known for being predominantly white – we've got a few schools where it is more diverse, but certainly on the outskirts of Bath, where I am, it's really low, really lacking in diversity. And it's so important that as professionals, we're having those conversations with children, we're showing pictures, we're talking about other things. We have books and we have resources that represent how diverse the rest of the country is. When we live in areas like this, we have a really big responsibility to think even more about diversity and representation. We need to be aware and think carefully about how we do that and what that looks like. Like you said, it is equipping our children. There is only 15 miles between my village and Bristol, and yet the difference between the two is huge. Often children don't leave this small area, they don't even go to Bath, which is six miles away, let alone Bristol which is 15 miles away. This is where school and nursery are so vital in opening up the world for children to see beyond their small community.

Jamel   You can see it. That's one of the things that kept me in the early years. Those interactions with children and making them know that there are people like me that do this work. We know that men only make up 4–5% of the workforce. And obviously when it comes to black men it's like 0.3%. And when children see me their interaction is so amazing. They want to know everything about me, they want to touch my hair, touch my beard, they ask me about my gold tooth. It's like they're shocked by me, it's like wow, like, this guy is a giant, but at the same time, he's so kind. He plays, he teaches me things and so on, and building up the bond and building up those relationships is so amazing. For me personally, it is one of the key reasons why I'm here, why I do what I do. In some communities, black men are not often looked at in the best way or in a positive light. And just being there as a sole role model, it does so much good. Even the other day, a parent said to me that their daughter saw a black man in Asda, and said, "There's Mr J, There's Mr J", and went up to try to hug that black man. The parents said, "no that's not Mr J", and they told me, and the little girl was laughing because she thought she saw me. Often children from white heritage wouldn't have interacted with a black man, a black person before, or within their social group or their family circle. So maybe now she's realising, wait a minute, there are other Mr J's out there. It's beautiful, it's such a beautiful thing. And even with this book, it is giving two different perspectives – me from the inner city as a black man and you living up in beautiful Somerset and swimming and doing all these things that you do. I just think it's so amazing and that's what makes what we're doing important. So important.

TIME TO REFLECT

- How do you create a space to enable children to take the lead? How do you follow their ques, prompts and interests to form a bond?
- How does your environment make children feel? Does it create a sense of belonging, safety and security?
- What ways do you help children to feel that they can trust you and that they are loved and welcomed by you?
- Think about a child who is finding it hard to settle in your setting. In what further ways could you help them feel they belong and help them to settle?

Reading for adults

Bottril, G (2018) *Can I go and play now: Rethinking the early years.* SAGE Publications.

Brown, B (1998) *Unlearning discrimination in the early years.* Trentham Books.

Cherry, L (2021) *Conversations that make a difference for children and young people: Relationship-focused practice from the frontline.* Routledge.

Csikszentmihalyi, M (2002) *Flow: The classic work on how to achieve happiness.* Rider.

Devarakonda, C (2014) *Diversity and inclusion in early childhood: An introduction.* SAGE Publications.

Ephgrave, A (2015) *The nursery year in action: Following children's interest through the year.* Routledge.

Grimmer, T (2017) *Observing and developing schematic behaviour in young children: A professional's guide for supporting children's learning, play and development.* Jessica Kingsley Publishers.

Grimmer, T (2021) *Developing a loving pedagogy in the early years: How love fits with professional practice.* Routledge.

Lane, J (2008) *Young children and racial justice.* 2nd ed. National Children's Bureau.

Mainstone-Cotton, S (2017) *Promoting young children's emotional health and wellbeing: A practical guide for professionals and parents.* Jessica Kingsley Publishers.

Murphy, K (2022) *Supporting the wellbeing of children with SEND.* (Little minds matter series). Routledge.

Murphy, K (2022) *A guide to SEND in the early years.* Featherstone.

🐛 Reading for children

Adeola, D (2021) *Hey you! An empowering celebration of growing up black.* Puffin.

Cahn, D (2019) *Umar.* Self-published.

Henry-Allain, L (2021) *My skin, your skin: Let's talk about race, racism and empowerment.* Ladybird.

Pascoe-Matthews , T (2020) *The Biggest Surprise: Jaden and the talking trains.* Self-published.

Tarpley, N (2004) *I love my hair.* Little, Brown and Company.

Building positive relationships with other professionals

In this chapter, Sonia and Jamel will be discussing:

- Working as part of a multi-disciplinary team; sitting with, understanding and respecting each perspective and area of expertise
- Having parents as part of the team around the child
- The importance of unifying the team around the child from the ground upwards
- Creating a shared understanding and breaking down barriers
- Bringing back the value of the practitioner and your position as an advocate for the children in your care
- Wellbeing of staff
- Empowering the practitioner and developing a supportive management structure and network
- The importance of having a diverse workforce and the need to diversify pedagogy and provision
- Men in the early years and issues with retention

DOI: 10.4324/9781003201373-3

Working in teams

Jamel   So, I think what's so important to understand is that everybody's perspective of the early years is different. Not everybody's going to see things the way you see things, not everybody's going to understand things the way you understand things, and not everybody is going to complete a task the same way that you will complete a task. And I think the main thing that matters is that everybody treats each other with respect because when it comes to supporting each other it's about using each other's strengths. There might be an area of expertise where I'm more knowledgeable or I've got more experience. Or there might be an area where you've got more experience. Two methods can work together to bring about the best outcomes, but sometimes that can get lost. Some leadership teams want to control individuals and make them feel insignificant, or like they need to paint themselves with the same brush that Dave painted himself with, that carbon copy. And that's not the way the world is. Not everybody is the same. We're all unique and we should all be embraced for our uniqueness and individuality.

Sonia   I wonder whether some of that is about control. I think we've both worked with people over the years where they're a bit of a control freak. And I hold my hands up and recognise I like to be in control. I'm a 49-year-old woman and there are some things I quite like to have some control over. But I've also learned that sometimes I need to let go, I can't control everything. Part of the joy of working with children is learning to let go of the control. You need to be able to learn to hold that balance and recognise in yourself when you are wanting to control things. We need to be able to stop and ask ourselves questions: What is my intention? Is this for me? Is this about my needs or is this about the needs of my staff or the children? Sometimes what we experience is people who feel insecure about themselves and their own knowledge, particularly if things are changing around them. For some people change can make them feel really scared, instead of being able to say, actually, this makes me feel a bit worried, and to be able to recognise their feelings and emotions. Sometimes they just don't have that emotional literacy and understanding and it can show itself through controlling behaviour, and like you said, they may try to force others to become a carbon copy of themselves. That is so hard for everyone.

Jamel   Definitely, because you will spend all your time trying to perfect yourself to meet someone else's standards and everyone's perception/perspective of perfect is different. Some people don't want to be perfect. Some people's best qualities are there in things that they find challenging. If all artists painted pictures the same way we'd have boring museums and boring art, the world would be a boring place. Some people use splatter, some people use strokes, some people use lines, some people use different types of geometrical shapes to paint pictures, but the thing is, the main thing is, that it is art, and the different types of art cater for different needs. Like you said, maybe some people just fear difference because they've never been around different types of people; they are used to working in one way. The thing that they have to understand is, especially in early years, this is not army barracks. We are not soldiers, we're not going to be marching every day. Yes, we follow a routine, but the routine is based on the flow of the child and based on their interests. So, if we've set up something or made different resources accessible for the children and they don't want to play with it, it's our responsibility as the supporting act in the situation to change what's there or point the children in another direction, so they're able to select their own resources or change or make those decisions themselves. It's the same with staff as leaders. We're supposed to give our staff, or our teams, the tools to make decisions themselves and to guide them. We need to have less of an authoritarian methodology of working and more of a ground-level leadership style, where you see things from the perspective of the people on the ground but, at the same time, you're able to kind of guide them based on your experience and knowledge with an expected standard.

Sonia   I've been a manager. I was a manager for three years but I am no longer in a management role; I'm now working with children and practitioners. I am advising but also directly working with the child, and I love it. I must admit I don't miss the management role! I think an important aspect of being a manager is supporting your staff and recognising the strength in your workers, but also being able to work together – learning together and reflecting on practice together. Also recognising when you can learn from your staff as well as them learning from you. When I was a manager I worked for a children's charity and my area of work was around children's participation. One of the staff I managed specialised in children with learning disabilities and at the time this was a new area to me, as my specialism was participation and I was running a participation project. I learned so much from her, from observing her practice, and she learned from me and my knowledge around participation. It was a two-way reflective and learning practice. I think it takes courage as a manager to acknowledge you don't have all the answers.

I think that learning from one another should be in all our work. I'm interested in how we do this as part of a team. I think we've both worked in multi-disciplinary teams. I currently work in a multi-disciplinary team. We have an education phycologist, a former head teacher, a former special educational needs co-ordinator (SENCO), a Forest School lead, a play and family therapist, someone who specialises in autism, and I have an early years specialism. So we are a really mixed bag. But we're all learning so much from one another. We regularly consult with one another to ask advice, get ideas. A key part of our role is to know that it's okay to not have all the answers and to go and ask others for their ideas and their support. For me that's a real joy about multi-disciplinary working. But I do know there are some teams where that is not a common practice – people work in their silos and don't share their knowledge. When we share and expand our knowledge, that's where we all learn so much more and it is beneficial for our children.

Jamel   Of course, and when you come from that kind of environment where you've got a multi-disciplinary team and everybody's there sharing, and then you go into an environment where that's not present, it's a shock to your system. Because everybody should be unifying under the heading of the child, TAC (the team around the child), and it's such a beautiful thing when it works out. I remember sitting down and having meetings with the SENDCO, the occupational therapists, the speech and language therapist (SALT) and social workers, and so on, saying, "Okay, where is the child in their development", and these different views or different observations marry, and then it's like, wow, okay, I thought that as well. And, when you're having these conversations you're just building on your knowledge and it's important that this way of working is something that we value because there's so much positive about that. I think it gets lost when practitioners and other professionals start competing, because sometimes you can have this multi-agency approach and everybody thinks they're right. I'm right. What I'm saying is right, I know more than you, but I spend more time with the child on a daily basis, you only see the child on the weekends, you only see the child in the evening, you only see them once every six weeks and so on. But when you marry it all together, there's so much value.

Sonia   It's about everybody listening to one another. Even if you're not completely in agreement. I have been working with a child recently where I saw them behave in a very different way to how other professionals had seen. A negative story had been created around him. I and his new setting were able to tell a different story. Thankfully, the other professionals were able to take on board and listen to what we were seeing, they were open to hearing a different story. Sometimes we need to stop and ask what is the story we have, is that the real story? Are we willing to have that story challenged? Or to change that story? Brené Brown has a really nice phrase that I like, I don't know if you're familiar with the work of Brené Brown? She is an inspiring woman. She is a research professor in Houston. She has a question: "What's the story in your head right now – is that the real story or is that a story you have created?" I find this so useful. Both for myself but also for the children I am working with. There have been many times when I have created a story in my head, maybe about a school I am working with or an individual, and I need to stop and ask myself that question.

Jamel   It's true, and asking and not being afraid to ask if you don't understand something or you've got something misconstrued about what someone's saying – ask. Reflection and asking are two important tools because sometimes we sit in our own space and we sit with our own thoughts creating stories. And a lot of the time they could be fictitious, based on our own anxieties, or you talk to someone and they can change the whole way that you see things. And I think the main thing I've got from what you just said is about the true picture of the child. The true image of the child. The true image of practice. And with that, we're able to unify and create a working style that suits everyone. Create an environment that has no bias, no judgement, just a level of respect, a child at the centre of our practice. That's the main thing: How does this benefit the child? How does this benefit us? How does this benefit the setting, and working alongside parents as well? People often forget that parents are the practitioners at home. So, with those parent relationships, we're then able to kind of get another perspective of the child because children behave differently at home to when they're in the setting. So, there may be particular foods or a particular way that they like to do things at home, and they'll do it differently in the setting because they're around their peers or they're around us.

Parents as part of the team around the child

Sonia Again, I think this comes back to listening. For me this is the underpinning foundation for everything we do – for our work with children, with our colleagues and with parents. Listening is so vital. One of my first jobs was working with children with non-organic failure to thrive. We worked with children aged 6 months to 3 years. They were referred to us as the children were losing weight, they were often refusing to eat or were eating limited food. On our first visit to the parents we were trying to find out about the family and history. A question I always asked was, "what is it that really scares you?" That was a heavy question to ask and often no one had asked them before. Commonly, the parents would say how scared they were and how they were afraid their child may die from not eating. That is hard to listen to and hard for the parents to say out loud. I learnt that sitting and listening and holding that space for them was so important. To acknowledge the pain and worry they had and to let them know I was there to support them and to help them to get their child to put on weight again. Often the story they had in their head wasn't what was going on, the children were often not at that point. But listening to them, giving them space to express that story, the listening was vital.

Jamel   Yeah, building those bonds. And like you said, sometimes we can be diving in giving advice, but just take a step back to gauge the temperature and learn who these people actually are. Then, and with that, you're then able to hold meaningful conversations that are not all about work, not all about development, not always sticking within the professional lands. Yes, be professional and have boundaries, but at the same time, have a personality. You like the football. Did you watch the football? Because then the parents are able to relax and then, with that, you can then ask those hard questions because they won't be so hard to hear. I think it's like breaking down the food, making it more digestible. The conversation is the food and just adding a bit of moisture to it makes it easier to go down and digest, because often parents have their back up, staff may have their back up, thinking why are they asking me these things, they have no right. But if you build that bond there'll be more willing to give and we've got to be willing to receive.

Sonia As professionals, we're asking an awful lot of those parents. We are expecting parents to put their precious children into our care. When I work with new children in September, I need to persuade their parents that I am going to love their child. I am going to do whatever I can to make their experience in school a really good experience. And that I am going to be their child's advocate. Some of the parents are anxious and worried about the child starting school. They might be concerned if the child will be violent and at risk of being excluded. That's scary for them – some parents can be prickly and shouty. As professionals we need to be able to recognise the story they might have in their head. It's okay to ask parents what they are worried about. Once we understand this, we are then in a better position to support them.

Jamel Once you get past that step, we're able to feed the information to the parents, to the teams, from different perspectives – from the personal perspective and from the professional perspective. And then everyone can kind of be on the same level. Oh, Mum and Dad don't like this, Mum and Dad prefer to be approached in this way. Mum and Dad are a bit anxious about this so when you feed back this information, this is the way that you deliver it, and it really brings back the whole importance of the key person, as well. Being key people and having that consistency. And when we talk to other professionals outside of the remits of the setting, we can say last week that they were going through this and this is how best to support them if they need help with a, b and c. I remember there was a child, he was putting on weight and he wouldn't eat healthy foods, it was all snacks and things like that. When it came to normal food, it was just plates on the floor and displaying challenging behaviours. He was on the spectrum and he wasn't getting enough exercise, and Mum was very anxious because he was a poorly baby. His start was challenging, and I just remember, daily, building up a relationship with Mum. And I remember when she had to see the onsite doctors and nurses had to weigh him and so on (health checks), I came in with her because she felt that sense of security with me present. And I remember she had to take off his trousers so they could check his legs because he wasn't walking, he was always putting himself on the floor all the time and wanting to be carried. She always had to support him with his clothing but with us the child wanted to be independent and do things himself. So we shared this and worked together – me, the teachers, teaching assistance, doctors and occupational therapists as well. And yeah, the child made leaps and bounds. So, it's so important to build up those bonds, build up a level of trust, and be able to give relevant feedback because, as I said, the parent did not know that their child could remove their clothes or undo fastenings himself.

Sonia Again, this comes back to working as a team, being part of that team. Seeing the parents as part of the team around the child is so essential. When we all work together as a team, that is powerful for the child and parents. Sometimes parents tell me the child can't do something at home and we can share how they can do it in school or nursery. At times like this I might say to the child, "Harry, I've been telling Mum how brilliant you are at putting your shoes and socks on at school because you do it really well. I wonder if you could show her how clever you are, I think she'd really like to see that". This is showing the child that we are all here working with them and that I know sometimes they do things within the setting that they won't do at home.

Jamel Exactly, exactly. And just bringing it back to the class-room, and the way staff work, and keeping things consistent – my method of working might be very different to the way another person might work. Someone might put on a child's jacket for them and put on their hat for them, and not create that opportunity for the child to do it themselves independently. Just based on maybe experience and the routine – the routines rigid so they don't have time to allow a child to take their time in putting on their coat, their trousers and so on. But that can cause segregation, those differences in opinions and views. Some practitioners, they don't like plastic. They only want natural resources. So, let's bring it back to that place and think about how we accommodate that. Because, as I said, everyone's experience is valuable. And it really is about having an understanding of the fact that we're all climbing the mountain, but there's different ways to get there, different ways to get to the top. And at the end of the day, having a child at the centre of our practice, they can benefit but there's moments where they don't because the needs of a child can change and the methods of teaching can change, with pedagogy becoming outdated. Yeah, especially with like a lot of the old-school methods.

Sonia I think sometimes we need to have those really uncomfortable conversations. Sometimes we need to name it and say if we need to make a change. I think a useful tool can be modelling change. Using the "I wonder" phrase can be useful – it's a phrase I use a lot with children but it can also be useful with colleagues: "I wonder if we tried something different today, it might not work but I would like to try it." Then implement the change and reflect together about it. But sometimes you just need to name it and say this isn't okay, we need to change this. Obviously, this would be done in an appropriate way – privately with that person. You may also need to go to their line manager. That's hard, but sometimes it is necessary.

Jamel That's because you put yourself in a position of vulnerability, no one likes to be told that what they're doing is wrong. No one likes to be corrected. And, some people, they're not confrontational or not confident to give that feedback, and that's where the role of room leaders and senior management definitely comes in. But at the same time, people don't want to be labelled as a person that goes to the office and reports, but if it's something that's a safeguarding issue or something that could create a possible safeguarding issue then it definitely has to be fed back ASAP.

Sonia   Absolutely, but also as well as safeguarding we sometimes need to try and encourage a change in general practice. One way I encourage people to do this is by seeing other people's practice – visiting other settings can be so useful. You won't like everything that they're doing, but there will be some things that you can learn, ideas you can get. That can be really useful. Every setting is unique, we can learn so much from seeing other practice. I am so fortunate in my job as I have many opportunities to see the practice of a wide range of settings. I am always learning and taking away new ideas. Another useful tool is using video, if you can be brave enough to video yourself or video your room and then rewatch it. In my old work with children with feeding difficulties we did this a lot. We would video ourselves and the children and then rewatch it as a team and unpick what was happening. At first this feels very odd, and you have to trust your team, but it's a useful practice. The reflective practice of looking at what you did and thinking about what worked and what could be changed. It can be very powerful and useful.

Jamel   Yeah, and just to go alongside with what you just said, peer to peer observations and sharing practice are brilliant. It doesn't always have to be the room leader, it could be just one of your colleagues or even a colleague from another room. When I've seen something that's amazing, be it online or on YouTube, I'm always sharing. Alright, I've got this video I've just seen. I'll go to another room and see a brilliant activity going on, guys, look at this, come, come, come. Look at this. Wow, this is amazing, and even if I've done something myself that's brilliant I would share with the other rooms. What happens is you create a culture where everyone's willing to go to each other, oh I've got this outcome that I want to meet, what activity can I do? I want to do a sensory activity, I want this, I want to do that. And then someone will come up and say, Oh, sensory story, that's brilliant, the child likes the bear hunt. Can you do a sensory activity with the bear or a sensory activity with 10 Little Fingers 10 Little Toes and the staff, they will benefit from it. As you said, we can be stuck in a setting for a number of years and think that this is it. And it's not because if you go to a Montessori nursery it's totally different or if you go to a Reggio Emilia, their practice is different as well.

Sonia   It's recognising how much more learning we can all still do and finding ways to do that. That might be through sharing ideas with team mates, visiting other practices, reading and sharing our reading with one another, learning from others in the field across the country and from other countries. I've been working in the early years world 30 odd years and I'm still learning new stuff, that's how it should be. The moment I stop learning it's time to leave.

Jamel   And if we're just sitting still, what happens to still water is it becomes stagnant, right, and we don't want to become stagnant in our practice.

Sonia   You can't swim in stagnant water.

Jamel   That's the thing. We want water that flows so we can flow. The other day I got sent a document, I think it was a music development matters document and I was just like, wow, like, I've never seen this before. This is all music and it's EY. This is brilliant. I mean, with these kinds of things we're just empowering ourselves, and then we're able to empower others, empower our teams, empower our colleagues. This empowers everyone, and it's just a beautiful thing. And like you said, you need to be prepared to listen. You need to be prepared to listen and you need to be prepared to act, but act in unison. It's not all about you, it's about moving as a team, and when we move as a team, then the movement's more impactful. It's like painting a wall. If you put one strip of paint on the wall, it's like, okay, you painted, you've done one strip. If you've got a small brush, it's like, it's just one strip. But if you've got a massive brush, and you all paint at the same time, you're going to have a beautifully painted room.

Jamel   What we're talking about is strategy. It's about having the right strategies in place. If you're coming from one direction a lot of the time you can miss, but if you're firing from more than one angle you are more guaranteed to hit something. That really needs to come from the top down, because if you've got a good leadership then you've got good role models to shape your practice and if you've got a toxic leadership team then your practice and perspective will become toxic because they're shaping the norms. The empowering of the practitioner comes from leadership. Also, making sure that your staff's wellbeing is catered to, because staff can become overwhelmed with information, rotas, with all these instructions and roles they have to play. They're hit with a list of things to do as well as working with the children.

Wellbeing

Sonia As you know, wellbeing of staff is a big part of the work I do. Unfortunately, this can become tokenistic. I can become quite worried when I hear about wellbeing weeks. They sound great in practice but have a danger of being tokenistic and then it's dropped. I'm much more interested in how we can embed wellbeing into the work practice. I know Kate Moxley has done a lot of work with settings around this. If your staff need breakfast then provide breakfast, not just for one week but do it all year. Your staff should have a decent staff room to take a break in and it should not be cluttered or have children popping in and out of it. It's their space to get away and have a break. It should be in place all the time. Also, as a manager, what are you modelling? So, if you are sending emails at 12 o'clock at night, what message is that giving to your staff? Head teachers are really guilty of that. It's not okay – what that says to your staff is, I'm working at midnight, why aren't you? That's not acceptable. Some questions to ask yourself are, What are you modelling? What are you sharing? Are you talking to your staff about how you look after yourself? Everyone that knows me knows I'm passionate about wild swimming, which is about looking after my wellbeing. I often talk about it with the staff I work with. By having these conversations I can hopefully encourage the staff to think about what they are doing for their wellbeing.

Jamel   Yes. Yes. Having that level of respect, you know, just in general chitchat and checking in on staff and really caring. One thing I would ban is these wellbeing questionnaires which you're obligated to fill in. And you cannot be honest, you know, especially if you're in a toxic environment. You feel like if you say something, your jobs on the line, and you're asked, oh, do you think that we cater towards your needs? Do you think the management provided for your wellbeing? Do you think this and the third? And you're having to put your name on the documents. I think that if it is something, if you're going to do it, make it anonymous and ask the questions in a way with some emotional intelligence.

Sonia   It's only worth doing them if you're going to act on it. Don't do it in a tokenistic way. It also needs to be within a safe environment.

Jamel   Yeah, of course. I've worked with a range of people – a range of black people, white people – and different settings – grass roots settings, inner city nurseries and then the more upper-class range of settings. And the main thing that I've found, the unified thing that I've found, is you cannot have a second run smoothly. If you are not actively looking after your staff's wellbeing, what you have is staff members calling in sick, staff members quitting, a high staff turnover. Lots of disciplinaries, a lot of staff not being able to fulfil their role wholeheartedly because they're just overwhelmed and not feeling themselves. You know, you see the strain, staff members crying, staff members not feeling listened to, but feeling obligated to stay because they've been there a long time. And that has a domino effect, which then affects the other members of staff – their wellbeing may not have been affected as much as those members of staff but what happens is they have to carry the workload left over, and things like that can be detrimental to your health, detrimental to the children. It is so disruptive and is something that all leaders, colleagues, people in positions of power, setting owners, doesn't matter if you're a PVI (Private, Voluntary and Independent) or government funded, you need to acknowledge this; wellbeing is the centre of everything.

Diversifying

Sonia   Diversifying is an interesting area for us to discuss. I live in Bath and North East Somerset, which is a predominantly white area. What I am going to ask is maybe a really naive question but we have talked about asking what we don't know. The area I live in is predominantly white, it's changing a bit but really slowly. Most of the workforce are white. But Bristol, only 15 miles away, is completely different, it's a wonderfully diverse area. As an education/early years sector, what can we do about actively recruiting more diversely? I know many settings who really want to do this but are struggling to know how.

Jamel That's a good question. So, basically, it's just understanding that I don't think diversifying the workforce is isolated to any particular area, I think it's the concept of the whole sector. So, for instance, there was a document written in Scotland, about diversity, and there wasn't any. Well, basically, the writers weren't diverse. They were talking about diversity, and it was a panel of white people. I've got a wide network of people, and I knew a lecturer, PhD student just finishing off his PhD, black, he's of black heritage, and he's in Perth, and I just put him through to them, and they were like, oh my gosh, we knew of this young man but we didn't think of him. So, it's about having the knowledge, widening your circles, widening your network, and knowing who's around. It's about your advertising – how do you show the world, show the people in these rural areas, that your setting is diverse?

Sonia I totally agree with that. And I've had those conversations in the past and in previous organisations I've worked with, but it's really breaking that down. How do you do that in a way that isn't tokenistic, in a way that is really genuine?

Jamel I think that it comes from having an understanding of the world. Having an understanding that outside of this rural area there is a more cosmopolitan society where there are different people from different walks of life, doing different things, enjoying different things, that look different, that have different preferences, and illustrating that in the nursery. It could be through music, it could be through food. It could be through books. It could be other resources. And not just doing it because you have those particular people in a setting but doing it because it illustrates a true picture of the world.

Sonia I agree, I think a lot of places are beginning to get better at that. In our local area we have an excellent charity called Sari, they have helped many organisations to think about this and change practice. I think it is the advertising for jobs that settings are struggling with, really being able to show we are wanting to recruit a diverse workforce. Thinking about the words you use in job adverts, thinking about how you actively show what will welcome people.

Jamel Yeah, when you look at a setting, and you look at the environment, and you see the pictures online of what the setting looks like you can see the aesthetic. And just, you get a general feel, and I think it's not even about specifically advertising that you are looking for "a male practitioner". No, it's about saying, well, we're an open environment that are looking to diversify our workforce and creating a welcoming environment that illustrates this to the world. We need to be more welcoming, we need to make people know that even though we're in a rural area, we welcome all, and we cater for all, and it's not tokenistic. For instance, you like swimming. Maybe you've gone to the Caribbean and swam in Dunn's River, swam in Trinidad Goo Goo patch river, you've gone to Barbados swimming in rivers over there, and you've put up pictures saying here is me swimming in the lake district but here's a picture of me swimming in the Caribbean, beautiful water. A Jamaican person will see that and say, oh, she's swimming in Jamaica. I want to meet this lady, she doesn't only swim in England. It's about using our interests but showing that there's different dynamics to who we are. I think sometimes we get caught up. Because diversity, inclusive practice, is such a delicate thing to cater to. So often people are scared to approach it, but it's about really being authentic, organic and real to yourself. We're going to find this challenging, but there's always something you can do. So, for instance, you're in a rural area, call someone like me, or Liz Pemberton or Joss Cambridge Simmons, or Shaddai Tembo, Laura Henry-Allain etc. Invite them in and say, look, we've got this setting, we want different types of people to come in and visit, and what you're doing is you're creating an experience for those children that they wouldn't normally have.

Sonia   Thank you, that's really helpful advice, and particularly the, "if you don't know go and ask somebody because somebody else will". Don't be afraid to say I don't know. Also being curious. So recently in the last few weeks I have a little boy whose grandparents live in Ghana, and he has just been so excited to show me Ghana on the atlas. It's just been wonderful having conversations about what he did there. We connected over swimming and food, he was talking about his experiences of swimming with his grandma in Ghana and the food they ate, and I was talking about swimming with my nan when I was a child, and swimming now and the food I ate with my nan. It was beautiful – a wonderful connection. I haven't been to Ghana, but that didn't matter. It was a great moment of learning, listening and being curious.

Jamel   That exchange, and what we're doing, is raising up cultural capital. It means we're sharing, we're exchanging where we're building that scaffolding and where we're breaking down the scaffolding. The world is a humungous place with so many different things happening. I want to explore it. I want to learn more. I want to listen. And then I want to go and experience it myself. And that's the beautiful thing man, the possibilities are endless. So, when it comes to having a diverse workforce, or having diversity within a setting, it starts within us, the practitioners – it starts within us.

Sonia   That's it, don't be afraid to be afraid about what you don't know.

Jamel   Dive in, dive in.

TIME TO REFLECT

- How can you use your strengths to collaborate with and support your colleagues? How can you use the strengths of your colleagues to further develop your knowledge and practice?
- In what way can you engage in purposeful, respectful and personal dialogue with your colleagues while maintaining a level of professionalism?
- How are you embedding a culture of diversity and cultural awareness in your setting?
- Is this an area in which you need some continuing professional development (CPD)?

Reading for adults

Brown, B (1998) *Unlearning discrimination in the early years*. Trentham Books.

Brown, B (2018) *Dare to lead*. Vermilion.

Brown, B (2021) *Atlas of the heart: Mapping meaningful connection and the language of human expereince*. Vermilion.

Campbell, J C (2019) Retention in the early years and why it matters. Available online at: https://my.optimus-education.com/retention-early-years-and-why-it-matters

Csikszentmihalyi, M (2002) *Flow: The classic work on how to achieve happiness*. Rider.

Henry-Allain, L and Lloyd-Rose, M (2021) The tiney guide to becoming an inclusive, anti-racist early educator. Available online at: https://assets.ctfassets .net/jnn9p19md0ig/4ntGEh21KNXyB9aLxq9gCY/618 47fa97f563ba4d9b281cf89d8a8ef/Guide_Inclusive_ Education.pdf

Mainstone-Cotton, S (2017) *Promoting emotional wellbeing in early years staff: A practical guide for looking after yourself and colleagues.* Jessica Kingsley Publishers.

Matthews, B (2005) *Engaging education.* Open University Press.

Moxley, K (2022) *A guide to mental health for early years educators: Putting wellbeing at the heart of your philosophy and practice.* Routledge.

Tembo, S (2021) Black educators in (white) settings: Making racial identity visible in Early Childhood Education and Care in England, UK, *Journal of Early Childhood Research*, 19(1). https://journals.sagepub.com/doi/full/10 .1177/1476718X20948927

Reading for children

Campbell, J C (forthcoming) *Olu's teacher.*

Building positive relationships with families and the wider community

In this chapter, Sonia and Jamel will be discussing:

- Parent partnerships
- Empowering families, listening to families and embracing their culture
- Building relationships with parents where there are difficulties at home
- Relationships with dads
- Working with parents who have fostered or adopted children and may be struggling to form attachments
- Creating a "circle of friends"
- Making community links
- Multi-generational approaches
- Celebrating diversity

DOI: 10.4324/9781003201373-4

Working with parents

Jamel   Parent partnerships are essential. Obviously, we're looking after their children, and children are very receptive of the vibe and of interaction and connection. And if the children don't see the practitioner/specialist getting along with the parent, the child can be apprehensive when it comes to developing a connection with the practitioner. I think parent partnerships are an important component of consistency and learning as well – so the practitioner knows what the parents are doing at home and the parents know what the practitioner is doing within the setting.

Sonia   It's that "joined up ness", isn't it; the message to the child, we're a team, your team. You are at the centre, and we are the people around you, and we're all working together. In September, a lot of people go back to schools and nurseries, and so a lot of new relationships are beginning. And it's about how you build those up and how you build that trust. It's a really big thing – if you send your little one into this other environment that isn't the home, you are trusting those adults. That they are going to love your child and care for them and nurture them. Yeah, that's a really big ask.

Jamel   Especially for first time parents as well. This is their first child, this is their precious cargo, and a lot of the time parents can be anxious because they're putting their child in an alien environment, and it says a lot about us, that we have to then initiate those conversations, make the environment warm and build those relationships with parents from the beginning. The settling in period, when you think about it, is a short space of time so it's very hard.

Sonia That's why I really like home visits. They used to be a really regular thing, certainly with children going to school. Home visits for that transition into reception was seen as good practice and I'd say most schools in our area will have been doing that for a long time now. Last year, because of COVID, it stopped. Now interestingly, this year, they've stopped it again. And they've blamed COVID. And I have to say I've challenged them, because this summer they could have done those meetings outdoors. The problem with not doing home visits is it's such a useful tool for helping children to feel settled and for you as practitioners to have a better understanding of what's going on at home and what life is like. So, if you've been to the family home, you've seen who lives there, how it is and where they live and, and it's a real honour to go into a family home. It really, really helps that transition, and I hope that by the time this book is published things have quieted down and people are going back to that good practice of home visits. It's an important part of our practice that I think we've lost and it's easy to kind of go, oh we don't need to do that, and it's like, no we do, we need that one coming back, we do.

Jamel It creates balance. In a setting I was working in previously they would often do home visits and they would talk about different resources that the parents have at home. Even the way that the properties are set out, the space that the child has, whether they have their own room, whether there is an outdoor area and so on. And then with that understanding, seeing them in their home environment, they were able to adapt that within the setting. If they have an exercise ball or if they've got like different sensory toys and so on, they were then able to say, okay, I noticed that at home. Let's adapt that within the setting. And the child seeing you in their home environment, it's like, oh, I've seen you before, you've been to my house. You've been there and it's good to make that crossover. I think with COVID the one thing I've really appreciated, even though it's been hard not having as much physical contact, was the Zoom sessions that we had – the one-to-one Zoom sessions. I think it helped parents to understand how much we do within a setting and also us as the practitioners to understand how much parents do at home. Because we would do different activities and we'd show our parents the structure of the day, be it circle times and then just doing different activities, like colourful semantics or coin recognition, or even just messy play and mark making and so on, and parents, they have this perception that there's this rigidity, there's a rigid structure, but them seeing us doing these sessions and seeing them in play, they were then able to understand that, wait a minute, there is a level of flexibility. So, yeah, we then gained a mutual respect, a higher respect, based on the interactions.

Sonia   I think the other key thing to think about when working with parents is whether our environment is welcoming to parents. In the current team I work for, one person is a former head teacher of an infant school – he used to run the nursery and then he became the head teacher. I recently interviewed him for my last book and he told me how they thought a lot about the space they provided for parents and how they wanted to ensure the space helped parents to feel welcomed. He also said if he needed to talk to a parent, he would rarely do it in his office. He was aware, for some people, it may have felt like they were coming to him to be told off. They had zones around the school and one of the things they did was put in benches, by herb areas and flower areas, so that adults could sit next to each other and have conversations. They also had a parent room – he recognised they were very fortunate to have the space to do these. That conversation raised some interesting questions for me. For some parents they bring their child to nursery or to school and they're really positive about it if their own experience has been positive, but a lot of the parents I work with, maybe they didn't finish their education or were thrown out of school. Maybe their school experience had been a nightmare. Or maybe they are anxious because their child has high needs and they don't know how those needs are going to be met in school. They could be coming to school or nursery with worries or preconceptions, which will colour their view of the school. As professionals we need to recognise that we know education because we live it and breathe it, but for other people it's really intimidating, and I think we need to ask the question, how can we make this more parent friendly and what does that look like?

Jamel Also, in the way that we talk, the language that we use. Often, that can be intimidating if we're talking to them in jargon and abbreviations and so on, our parents are looking at a us like, pardon? They're not professionals, and that's where the whole key person approach comes in because then that parent has that consistent face, a person that really knows their child and a person that they can really turn to – that go-between that can give genuine, knowledgeable feedback to the rest of the team and hold those difficult conversations. I've also found that dads, especially with our dads, some of them find it really difficult. As we know, the sector's majority of the workforce is female and some dads find that intimidating. They're not used to being in that kind of environment, and having staff that they can connect to, people that they can relate to, actually helps to bring them into the settings. So often when I talk to my dads I'll be like, "Come in, come inside", because a lot of them, they'll just be at the door. It's about that encouragement, and often you see that they do connect with the male members of staff. They'll be a bit warmer, a bit more friendly, and I've had that feedback from members of staff like, oh, Johnny's dad, he talks a lot to you, but he hardly talks to me, and so on. So, yeah, that says a lot as well I think about having a welcoming environment. And just encouraging our parents to come inside and showing off what their child's done as well.

Sonia   Yeah, it is so important for us to show a genuine interest. Even remembering those little things, "oh did you have a good weekend away?", that goes a long way. It is part of building a relationship and trust. That then helps a lot when you need to have a more awkward conversation. The thing about dads I think is really interesting. I'm aware a third of our team are men and that's unusual because we all work with reception class children and, as we know, men are hard to find in reception classes. We need more men in early years. I don't know how we change that but, well there's lots of ways to change it, but we need more men.

Jamel   We do, we do, we do, there's so many directions that can go, but I think, in general, to help build up those relationships within the community and encourage more people to join our early years workforce, it's the exposure. People have this misconception of what early years is and what a nursery is – this holding bay where children are kept so people can work and so on, rather than an institute of learning. They think that the learning goes on in the primary stages and so on. But it's about us promoting and profiling and being present within our communities to encourage more people to join the workforce and help with the relationships we have with our existing parents, because word of mouth is the biggest promotion tool and nurseries are the hub of the community. So parents should know a little bit even before they've done their research on the internet, "oh this nursery, my neighbour's child went there"

and such, and this is what they said. So, it's about us just being present, being available and inviting people in.

Sonia   Definitely, just one thing I want to add on the parent work. Some of the most inspiring work I know of with parents is from Pen Green's work. They've been going around for a long time. Originally, they were a sure start centre and they have a nursery based there. Margy Whalley's book (2017) about working with parents is still one of those books I go back to again and again and again. I particularly love their work around schemas and how they involve parents in research. Research with parents is so exciting. Pen Green's research with parents, particularly around schemas, is ground-breaking. I mean, they've been doing it for years, about 20 years, but it still feels radical. They involved parents in research projects about their children's schematic interests. They gave parents cameras and encouraged them to take photographs and videos of their child's schemas. Together they learnt more about the child's interests, and I have heard interviews with parents talking about their knowledge of their child and the things that they've put in place now they understand about the child schema. I've heard an interview with a dad talking about fishing with his son and how it linked with his son's trajectory schema. He described the actions of throwing out the line, pulling in the rod, pulling in the fish, chopping the head off and gutting it. I am not a fishing person, but he explained how that all linked with his son's trajectory schema. It was just brilliant, it was beautiful and fantastic to hear. I found that level of involvement with parents inspiring.

Jamel   Even when having a meeting with parents' or just a pedagogical conversation at the end of the day of what their child's done, I've often brought up schematic behaviour because sometimes parents will have concerns about their childhood: my child keeps on throwing, my child keeps on putting toys into the DVD player or into the radiator and so on. And then I am able to have a conversation and explain what is actually schematic behaviour rather than challenging behaviour. When you build up that rapport and build up that understanding with your parents, they're like, oh, he's done it again. Now he's lining up toys or now he's doing such and such. And just off the back of what you said about Pen Green – I think it was in the 60s, the Plowden Report (1967). I remember that they adapted the Scandinavian way of practice and they would involve the parents – they would stay during the day to support the practitioners and work alongside the children.

Working with the community

Sonia   That reminds me of Reggio Emilia.

Jamel   Yes, it's amazing that community-based learning. When we're in the Caribbean, a lot of our learning is done outside and you could be walking past your child learning outside, and you can sit down and watch the class or join in, depending on what they're doing. Parents play an integral part of the learning as well, especially with the agricultural side of things, where there'll be growing food, fishing, even if it's just feeding the chickens before going to school and so on, but then you will go into school and then learn about agriculture as well. So, parents and teacher working hand in hand, and that Reggio approach is amazing.

Sonia It's so exciting to see. Seeing other practice is an amazing opportunity. I have been really fortunate to go on study tours to Reggio Emilia, Denmark and Sweden. Observing practice and having professional conversations with people from other parts of this country and overseas is so beneficial. Some things you want to try and implement and others you dismiss. In Reggio they describe a community of learning. I worked with one setting here and they wanted to have a community of learning around them. They contacted all their local businesses and asked if they would be part of their community of learning. The local businesses agreed. When they needed more knowledge, they would contact one of the community. There was one brilliant story, one summers day a child came into nursery and said, "dogs like ice cream, my dog's been eating ice cream because it's really warm". And somebody else said, "Well dogs can't eat ice cream". So, as a group, the children decided, okay, we're going to do an experiment to see if dogs like ice cream. They found out who had dogs and agreed it wasn't a good idea to bring them in at the same time as they might fight. Over a few weeks they brought in a dog, a day at a time. They went out to the shops and bought ice cream, they bought, vanilla, chocolate and strawberry flavours, and they put them in bowls for the dogs. They did a tally to see which ice cream the dog ate. They discovered that dogs like strawberry ice cream best. One child still kept saying that dogs aren't supposed to eat ice cream. As a group they discussed what to do. They remembered the local vets were in their learning community and wrote to the vet about their experiment and explained that "Peter says dogs shouldn't eat ice cream". They asked the vet for their thoughts. The vet wrote a letter back, and sent them a book, saying it was an interesting experiment but dogs shouldn't eat ice-cream as it's not good for them. She told them to look at the book for some ideas on how to look after dogs. I love that story. It was so inspired from the Reggio way of working, following children's interest. I mean, who in their right mind is going to do a project on dogs liking ice cream. Following the child's interest, involving the local community, enabling children to ask questions and find out, and it's just brilliant, isn't it!

Jamel   It's amazing, and then you have that whole multi-generational way of working, and you're teaching the children as well as learning yourself. As practitioners, we're always learning. We were doing a planting activity in a setting I was working in in Blackheath, and we would just go around the community exploring different plants, different seeds and so on, and we found this amazing florist, lots of different flowers, different colours, and then we went in there and they donated some flowers to us and said that anytime we wanted we could go in for the clippings. And then we stumbled upon this lovely greengrocers with these exotic fruits in, and the children were like, oh, fruits have grown too, so I was like yes. So we went in there and we got dragon fruit – they called it a dragon's egg – and so on. And then pomegranate and mangoes, and obviously some children have only seen the mangoes cut up, so we got different types – baby mangoes, long mangoes, Julie mangoes and so on. And then they explored the different purposes for the fruits, the different purposes for flowers – why do people have flowers? – and the activities just went on and on and on. The children then gave that feedback to their parents and told their parents, "Mom, we had dragon fruit today and this is where we got it from". And we went to the shop and then the parents started going into the shop as well. Right, and then they gave us feedback and said, oh, it was amazing, we knew the trip was happening but we didn't know that you were going to the greengrocers as well – we'd expanded it. And from that, parents would then go into different shops and buy different fruits themselves.

Multi-generational links

Sonia   That's fantastic and I guess that's probably what many other cultures do. We've just lost that here. Like you said, in the Caribbean, that's probably really an embedded part of what goes on. Sadly, we seem to have lost that connection. I think we need to familiarise ourselves with our community. We need to think about who our community is. It makes me think about the TV programe *Old People's Home for 4 Year Olds.* Did you see it? Alistair Bryce Clegg was one of the advisors re the children. I loved the joy it brought to both the children and adults. It was brilliant.

Jamel   When I was working in the House of Commons nursery we used to take the children at least twice a month to the old people's home, and it brought them so much joy. The children used to sing and play games, and it would only be for around about half an hour to an hour, but it was so nice for them to have that interaction, especially during Christmas. When we used to talk to the managers of the nursing home they said that the senior citizens were so excited to hear that the children were coming, and the children were so excited to go down there. "Oh yeah, I want to make a card, I want to draw a picture", and so on, and the children would sit so nicely and interact and talk and just build relationships, and have an understanding that, we're babies, and this is what can happen with time.

Sonia   Yeah, and I think particularly so with many of our families. Many don't have extended families living near them so rarely see grandparents.

Jamel   Yeah, because everyone's moving away, especially with the price of living going up at a rapid rate. A lot of people can't afford to live in inner cities, so they're moving further out, and often you find with that distance, there's a breakdown in communication. And just saying it, like me coming from the Caribbean, a lot of the elders and our families, they have gone back home, they live in the States, Canada, or somewhere else. They're spread all over the world. We obviously have the internet and so on, but with the internet, phone numbers can change and the internet can break down and so on, and you don't have that connection. So our children, well some of them are not getting that experience. Some of them are not getting the experience of interacting with the elders, which is an opportunity missed, but with nursing homes and such it's just such a beautiful thing.

The joy it gives you; how do you say it – when we sit down and observe children and the things that they say and the way they do things and the way they interpret the wider world, it's with such innocence and it's the same with the older generation. There's no filter – they just say what they see – and there's so much beauty in those relationships. And what we find as well is that the flip side to the paradigm of children not connecting or seeing their grandparents is there's some grandparents that raise the children that are present, and I think it gives them an extra lease of life.

Sonia   Over the years I've worked with a lot of children who've been raised by grandparents for a whole variety of reasons. And that can bring some wonderful things, but it can also be a real challenge. I must be honest, I'm nearly 50 and I can't imagine looking after a baby or a toddler at this stage in my life! It's hard work. The grandparents I've worked with have just been amazing, they've brought up their grandchildren because their children couldn't. There are some amazing grandparents.

Jamel   Sonia, what comes to the forefront of my mind is understanding that there are different households. And there are different types of people that are raising children, be it through the foster system, or co-parenting, single parents and so forth, and it's about us having an understanding of how all these different relationships and all these different dynamics actually help us in practice. To find the best ways to support and have an openness, because sometimes, we can come in to a setting and have our own present conceptions and perceptions of the world. And when we have these different people that come into the setting, we must be open minded of the wider community and the way things are.

Sonia   I think it's also having that curiosity, and I think it's also important to be able to very gently ask those sensitive questions. A lot of the children I work with are either in special guardianship, where grandparents or aunties are taking them on, or they're fostered or adopted. It's important in my first visits and conversations with the carers to be able to ask about the story of how the child arrived to them. It's useful for us to know but also to be able to understand how it has been and what it is like now, because that will then inform us more about what might be tricky for the child. That's not to say that we're viewing that through a deficit model but it's recognising that, if the child has had a difficult

71

start in life, that will potentially trigger other difficulties along the way. Even if now they are in a loving, safe place. We might especially see difficulties when there are big changes, such as moving to school or moving into a new room at nursery. Sometimes as practitioners we are afraid to ask the trickier questions. And my message would be don't be afraid, we can ask them in a gentle and sensitive way. Often, I will start my conversation with a new parent and I'll say, "I'm just going to be nosy, but it's just really useful for me to ask you some questions. If you don't want to talk about it, that's fine, but I am just going to ask a few things to help me understand your little one a lot better". By asking these questions gently and sensitively, in my experience, people are glad that you want to know and appreciate that somebody has taken the time to find out. You make it clear you're not judging them – it's about understanding so you can help their child better. It also enables you to find out if they talk about the birth parents, what they do for mother's/father's day, what the child calls them etc.

Jamel   Do it sensitively, that is so important. And I feel like what you've addressed is the fact that getting to know a child and getting to know a family is not paper based. Sometimes we can read these reports and application forms and think, okay, this is the picture of the child, but it's actually talking to the parents, talking to the child and listening, being prepared to listen and really take in that information. This is the dynamic, this is the ecological view of the child, who they are and what it is like at home, and what they've been through, and these are the things I can do to support them. In the new framework they talk a lot about communication and the importance of connecting and understanding different cultures and where children come from. It could be simple things, like understanding that in some cultures they eat with their hands or they prefer to sit on the floor and eat and so on. That helps our practice and that helps us not to make assumptions on where the child is in their development and who they are. They're showing us who they are, but to an untrained eye, it can look like something else.

Sonia   And I think along with that is again that whole thing about asking questions and being curious – I think it's important to not be afraid to ask. If you don't know, that's fine, ask about it. If you don't know anything about Ramadan, ask. Because actually the families are delighted to tell you – from my experience they love to be able to share something about their culture and about what they do and what they celebrate. But we, we need to show that curiosity. We have touched on this in the previous chapters, but I think sometimes we're afraid to ask questions, we're afraid to be curious. And because we're afraid that we're going to look stupid or maybe people are going to judge us, then we hold back. It's okay, being curious is good, it's okay to ask sensitively.

Jamel   It's so true, because what happens then, we've got all these thoughts that bubble up in our head and then we end up thinking in a discriminatory way, we're making these assumptions and then we're treating the child unfairly based on these thoughts, and that is ignorance.

So, we need to be brave, we need to be sensitive, and we need to explore –we need to be willing to jump in and swim.

And another thing that comes into play is having emotional intelligence – dipping your toes in and checking the temperature first.

Sonia   And you can tell immediately if you've gently asked something and it's not gone down right. You react to that and kind of jump in and go, okay, maybe that's not the question to ask, maybe we can look at this another time – and that's okay too.

Jamel   So, one thing that we have to work on, which helps parent relationships, is understanding the cultures around us, and not just celebrating cultures because the calendar says so. Following these annual themes – Hanukkah, Diwali and Kwanzaa, and all these kinds of things – and actually celebrating culture because we want to, we're intrigued about other ways of life, the environment and making links.

Celebrating diversity

Sonia   Yes, and involving the families in that. In one school I worked with, it was a new school, they started with the reception class and then would add a class each year, and grow the school that way. In their first year they had an interesting diverse mix of children from different cultures, which for our area is unusual. They decided to celebrate a rich variety of festivals, but with a big focus on the festivals the families celebrated. There were two Syrian families in the school and when it came to Eid the families made a feast for the school community. The whole school was just ten children plus three staff, so a small number. Everyone joined in the celebration, all the children, parents and staff eating and celebrating with one another. The children from the family were involved in making the food and then telling everyone about the festival, the food and why they were celebrating. It made it meaningful for everyone, and the children's self-esteem blossomed in the experience.

Jamel   I worked in a setting where there was only one black child, one black child in the setting. And we would do a cultural month. So, we had different foods, different traditions, different interests, it could have been football, music etc. And I remember we took ten children down to Elephant & Castle market and the children, they were excited to see the green bananas, saying "green bananas. What are green bananas?" I told them; you can eat green bananas. The little boy that was the only black child was so elated, he was picking up yams and sweet potatoes and showing his friends, and it was a lovely outing. When we spoke to the parents of the child they were so happy and they shared with us different places within Westminster where you can still get these kinds of foods and things like that, because we had to go to Elephant and Castle, but he was talking about all the places that they shop, and different things and he was so happy. The children were so happy because then they were able to use their new-found knowledge and experience and share it with their parents. Talking about the different squashes, pumpkins and plants in all these different kinds of foods, and sharing this information. And, man, we live in a cosmopolitan society. There's so much colour, so much music, so much culture. It'd be a shame if we just enclosed ourselves and didn't explore what was out there.

Sonia   But it needs to be embedded. I have concerns around how we do celebrate a week of something, for example, we're going to do black culture week. There's a real danger with those things of being tokenistic. We need to embed these things, we need to have it as a part of our culture, as part of what we do all the time, that we live and breathe, and not just, oh look, its black culture week, let's put out some pictures of black people. We need to change this way of working.

Jamel   Yes, even with our literature. You go into some of these rooms and you look at their libraries and it is just like, okay, you've got Handa's surprise, brilliant, but what else do you have? There's such a variety of books out there from different cultures.

Sonia   Yeah, a growing variety – there are so many lovely new books that are coming out all the time, celebrating a wonderful mix of diversity – we all need to go and get them.

Jamel   Talk to your parents, talk to your parents, because the parents will know about books you wouldn't know, be it *So much* or be it *The proudest blue,* etc. Parents will know and have these books at home and be able to recommend something to you, and that conversation, as you said before, being brave enough to say to parents, what can you help me with?! What music do you have at home? What books do you have at home? What foods do you cook at home?

Sonia   It's about being brave. I was in the greengrocer the other day, they were selling yam, an old black guy bought the biggest yam I have seen. I turned to him and said, "I have no idea how you cook that, can you tell me?" He was delighted to tell me. He told me about what he does and what his wife does with yam and the best ways to cook it and how it tastes and what to have with it. I had no idea, and that's all right. It was a great conversation.

Jamel   I've seen that with my nan in our local community in Catford, a lot of the elderly people, they grow, they've got the allotments, and they grow different things. And often people will come and bring things to the house. My nan was like, what's this, especially one time there was a huge butternut squash one of our neighbours gave to us, and she was like, Jah, how do you cook this. And I said, nan, it's just like a pumpkin, same way, take out the seeds and you can boil it, you can stew it and so on, and she was genuinely confused. And it's so funny. And then from that day she learned how to cook butternut squash, and this is the person that grows her own pumpkins, her tomatoes etc, but butternut squash was foreign to her. So, as she was sharing there's the exchange of language, and even in the Reggio Emilia approach, it talks about the 100 languages. Imagine the conversations that our children are having based on the dynamics that they come from. And then there's the whole billion-dollar word-of-the-moment which is cultural capital. Each child sharing different things from their cultures and creating an exchange, an environment that is diverse in knowledge. I know about yam, I know about planting; well guess what, I know about potatoes, and I know about, etc, and it's brilliant.

Sonia   But also, what it then does is it helps children to realise that other is okay. I was listening to an audible book, I don't know if you've read it but there's a new book by Oprah Winfrey and Dr Bruce Perry called *What happened to you?* – it's brilliant. In one section they are talking about racism. Oprah was asking questions around why there is racism. Bruce was saying that one of the big things is that if we're not used to being with others, we're not used to other, then you see the other as a threat. But once we begin to learn and ask questions and become familiar, it is no longer a threat. And that's what we need to enable with our children, to be able to see that other is okay. It might look different to me, but that's okay. And that's about, like you said, the food and the things that we experience, but also visiting. Over the years I have worked a lot with travellers, both new travellers and Irish travellers, and occasionally gypsy families. Sometimes in the school where my children went to, where I was on the chair of governors, we had new traveller children coming in and out. Sometimes the school would take the whole class (they were small classes) to go and visit the traveller site – see the trailers or vans they were living in and understand that it's okay, it's just different. They would notice what was different and what was the same, and it helped them to know that different is okay and that it doesn't need to be scary – we don't need to judge them, we don't need to be frightened, there's nothing frightening here, they just live differently. It was through the experience of seeing and realising it's okay, and then, like you said, they can go home and talk to their parents. And the parents as well need to realise that it's okay and that we don't need to be scared when there are travellers around.

Jamel Exactly, exactly. And then, when you have things like parents' evenings or events, parents are not so apprehensive to interact with each other. Because what often happens is children will have a relationship within the setting that they would want to extend outside of nursery but, based on those preconceptions, it causes some kind of friction with the parents interacting and making a decision with them, saying that "Tommy, you can go to Ellie's party" or "you can't". So, there's a wider picture with the work that we're doing, so we're not only empowering our children and creating these positive attitudes, but this is extended to the parents as well.

Sonia How change happens. That's how hopefully this will help to bring change, and to be more tolerant, loving and accepting – that's what we need.

Jamel   Be like the children – they're perfect in all their glory. They don't see the world in the way that we see the world, but through their eyes. That honesty is something that we can all learn from – the government, the world leaders, they just need to be in a nursery, as maybe through that lens we will be able to make real change. Yeah, because we forget what it's like to be a child. But parent relationships are so important. And I think something that we're learning more about daily. For us, the biggest lesson as well is being a parent yourself in some kind of context, be it uncle, auntie, extended family member – just looking after children of your own, having your own relations, can really help your perspective, so when you're then on the other side of the fence, being a professional, you can then work on your approach.

TIME TO REFLECT

- Does your setting have an anti-racism policy and inclusion policy? If not, how do you go about creating one? How may these policies help relations within and outside of your community?
- How do you accommodate your families, and their cultures and beliefs, and make them feel welcome?
- How do you help parents feel they are welcomed and listened to in your setting?
- How confident are the practitioners in your setting at working with parents? Is this an area you need some CPD around?

- What are your connections with the local community? Is this something you could develop further?
- Do you have safe spaces for parents to voice their opinions and be heard?
- How do you support and build the confidence of your parents to become involved in their child's learning and development (both at home and in the setting)?

🦋 Reading for adults

Akala (2019) *Natives: Race and class in the ruins of empire.* Two Roads.

Arnold, C and the Pen Green Team (2010) *Understanding schemas and emotion in early childhood.* Sage.

Blatchford, I S and Clarke, P (2000) *Supporting identity, diversity and language in early years.* Open University Press.

Brown, B (1998) *Unlearning discrimination in the early years.* Trentham Books.

Cherry, L (2021) *Conversations that make a difference for children and young people: Relationship-focused practice from the frontline.* Routledge.

Edwards, C, Gandini, L and Forman, G (2011) *The hundred languages of children: The Reggio Emilia experience in transformation.* 3rd ed. Praeger Publishers.

Mainstone-Cotton, S (2021) *Supporting children with social, emotional and mental health needs in the early years: Practical solutions and strategies for every setting.* Routledge.

The Plowden Report (1967) Children and their Primary Schools: A Report of the Central Advisory Council for Education (England). Available online at: http://www.educationengland.org.uk/documents/plowden/plowden1967-1.html

Whalley, M (2017) *Involving parents in their children's learning: A knowledge sharing approach.* Sage.

Winfrey, O and Perry, B (2021) *What happened to you? Conversations on trauma, resilience and healing.* Bluebird Books.

To watch:

Old people homes for 4 year olds. Available online at: https://www.channel4.com/programmes/old-peoples-home-for-4-year-olds

Reading for children

Adeola, D (2021) *Hey you! An empowering celebration of growing up black.* Penguin.

Cherry, M (2019) *Hair love London.* Penguin.

Cooke, T (2019) *So much.* Walker Books.

Cooke, T (2020) *Full full full of love.* Walker Books.

Love, J (2019) *Julian is a mermaid.* Walker books.

Muhammad, I with Ali, S K (2020) *The proudest blue.* Walker Books.

Watson-Senyah, R (2020) *The ABC of African and Caribbean food.* Self-published.

Conclusion

Sonia   Where are you living at the moment? Where's home for you?

Jamel   Ok, Catford. Yeah, so that's in Lewisham borough. Born, bred and raised. It's just amazing, going out for lunch and just being local. Whereas before, I missed out so much working in central London, working in East London, working in North London and so on, it's just been crazy. When's the last time you worked in an inner city?

Sonia   Me, I haven't. Actually no, that's not true, really early when I was training I worked in Bristol. But mostly I have worked in small towns or rural. Bath, rural Wiltshire, Somerset. So yeah, I'm the real opposite, I'm a rural woman.

Jamel   And so, like, that's amazing, because the way you're so in touch. And I think once you understand people, once you understand children, and once you've got a certain level of practice, it can be applied in any dynamic.

DOI: 10.4324/9781003201373-5

Sonia   It can, but what has made a real difference for me in my career was in one of my first jobs. I worked for a large national children's charity, the Children's Society, and I was based in Wiltshire. And then I worked for them in Bath, and then worked with them in Somerset and Dorset. Because they were a large national organisation, we did a lot of work across the country. So even though we were based in a rural area, we did a lot of learning from our colleagues. Also, for a while, back in the sure start days, The Children's Society used to run children's centres and I delivered the training to all the children's centres across the country on listening to children. So, I would travel from Leeds and Bradford down to Plymouth across to Portsmouth, all over. Of course, the beauty about that meant that I was seeing practice, diverse practice, from literally across the country. I realise now that's quite unique, early on in your career you don't normally get that, so I was really lucky.

Jamel   Yeah, and I think for myself similar. Not as vast, but meeting up with different men, like men in early years meetings, and different seminars or webinars. I was then able to kind of conversate and see where they were coming from and understand different dynamics, different setting layouts, and different ways that men – or practitioners in general – were working with children. Because of my practice and confidence they would often send me to different settings, so sometimes I'd be in an inner-city setting, and then they'd send me to Reading, or I'd be sent to Kingston or Richmond, or even meeting the guys from Bristol and the guys from Southampton, like the paint pots guys, seeing them and conversing with them. And then there were the other practitioners that came from Montessori nurseries and Reggio Emilia nurseries, and just building those relationships and developing my understanding of practice. So, when I look at things, just like you, we look at things with a wider scope.

Sonia   I think that's interesting, but I think it's also easy for us to take that for granted and kind of presume that's what everybody has, and then you realise, actually, no. I know people who have stayed in the same setting for 10–15 years, and that's fine, that's ok. But it's quite limited experience, that's why I'm always encouraging settings to go out and see their neighbouring setting, go to the neighbouring town and see if they can visit. Because actually, it's healthy to see different practice and hear about different practice, and then, internationally, if you get the opportunity to do it internationally, that is so worth it. It's just brilliant.

Jamel   Yeah, I've spoken to colleagues that have worked in Asia, worked in Sweden and Switzerland, all over the place, even in Africa, and they've told me, wow, like, that there's some amazing things that different people do, and I think that in itself is beautiful, when they bring in those stories to you and you're just able to develop ideas, develop different approaches. They had their lessons outside, or they had their lessons by a river, or their lesson consisted of them going on a nature walk, and that was the day. It's so amazing. And yeah, I agree that we can take things for granted.

It's about sharing that with our colleagues and saying there are different methods of doing the work out there that are as effective as what we do, and there's no confines and restrictions or caps to practice – it is an ongoing process of learning.

Sonia   I think being willing to be curious and ask questions, which is what we said all the way through this isn't it. I think that's probably been a running thread through our book, be curious, ask questions – to do with the children or the families or your colleagues, but also other practice – don't presume that the way you do it is the only way to do it. I'm working with a little boy at the moment who really struggles with the idea of children who he thinks aren't as clever as him. I'm working with him around the idea of diversity and what that looks like, and the fact that we're all different and that's ok. We all have different strengths and weaknesses, and that's ok, and it's all right to be different and ask questions. If I can get him to understand that at five (and it's proving to be quite tricky at the moment!), but if I can help him with that, he will have a great life skill there. It's the same for all of us, isn't it? It's ok, we're different and that's ok, that's good, let's celebrate that difference. That's what this book is. I really hope this book has shown that – you've got a middle-aged white woman and a cool black man, and we are different. But that's great, let's celebrate those differences.

Jamel   Yeah, yeah, and embracing it. It's such a beautiful thing that when we converse, you're seeing things and I'm smiling, and I'm seeing things and you're smiling, and we're bouncing off each other – that whole sharing practice thing where we're able to collaborate in such an amazing way and create something that is new. Yeah, it's not one-sided. It comes together in such a beautiful way. And even that in itself is a celebration; we're celebrating each other. I'm acknowledging you, you're acknowledging me and my practice, and through that we're building a bond.

Sonia Yeah. Which is good, we need more of that within the workplace and within the early years. I think sometimes in early years we can be in our own little silo, but also sometimes it can feel quite competitive. And it can feel like, oh, I've got my bit and my bit is children's wellbeing and my bit is adult wellbeing and this is my narrow bit and I don't know if I want to share that. But there's room for all of us, and let's just encourage one another. I think that's what I'd like to see more of – encourage the people who are reading our books, encourage the people that we work with, encourage one another. Yeah, there's a place for all of us.

Jamel I just hope that this book inspires, because there's so many of us that are scared because of those factors you stated before – the competition, the pressures, looking like a lesser academic than some or seeing ourselves as more of an academic than some. Yeah, and then the ego causes that conflict right. Where you then think, I don't need to do this, I don't need to collaborate with anyone, I don't need to talk to anyone, I don't need to communicate with anyone. I'll just sit on my own. On my own island and do what I've always done.

Sonia Yeah, definitely. I think the academic is an interesting strand. I don't know how you got into it, but I started in early years at 16, back then the qualification was an NNEB, which doesn't exist anymore. I did an NNEB for two years and then worked in a variety of roles. It wasn't until I was in my 30s that I went to do an early years degree. And I thought I was stupid, I had really struggled in school, but I had a lot of experience and I ended up discovering I could do it, and I wasn't stupid, and I did know stuff. And then I loved it – I got my degree and then went on and did an MA, and then, a few years later, I ended up writing books. So now I'm in a position where this is my ninth book and my books are on degree courses. I never in a million years thought that would happen. But it's amazing what can happen, what possibilities can be out there. When we can be brave enough to think I might try that. For me, doing a degree was brave, I had no idea if it was going to work out but I thought I should try. At the time I had two young daughters and I wanted them to know it was okay to go to university when you're 30 with children, while working and doing a million other things. It's possible and we can try new things. And now I have daughters who are doing MAs and considering PhDs – that's encouraging. That's inspiring. But yeah, give things a go, and if I'd given it a go and it didn't work out, that would have been okay too.

Jamel   Yeah, and that's just like my journey into the early years, just starting off by being called into a youth club, by chance. My uncle happened to be the one that was running it and he was my mentor. And he said, come in, try this youth club stuff because all the kids in the area, they know you, so come and support me. And then he said why don't you go into your qualification and then, from doing the qualification, I then stumbled into the early years and never looked back. I did a Cache certificate in preschool practice first, level two. And then I was working at an after-school club, and then after the after school, well I worked at sure start first, and then the After School Club, and then from the After School Club got taken on by Casterbridge and from Casterbridge got my level three, and I never thought of myself going in again and studying because I didn't like school. I didn't like it, but I loved reading. I loved literacy, and not even literacy like these big textbooks or anything like that as children's books. So, and if you remember the old-school early years books, they had a lot of diagrams and pictures, and I just loved it. I looked at it and was like, wow, this is something I could do, this is something I understand, and I made that connection. Here I am years later – I started at the age of 15. Wow, it just feels crazy, 20 years later, doing all the things that I'm doing.

Sonia   Great. Yeah.

Jamel   It's a blessing.

Sonia Because they're two different journeys and that's brilliant. We all bring such a wealth, like the people who are reading this, everybody brings their own wealth of stuff and we need to be proud of that.

Jamel And it just makes you think. I think this book overall will make you think about the relationship that you have with the early years itself and why you joined the sector, why you do what you do and what actually makes you good, what made you stay – because as we know, this sector is not a sector for those that want financial gain, and this sector is not for the light-hearted either. There's good days and there are hard days – hard, testing days.

Sonia Yeah, I think also what's exciting about this sector is that you can often just think, early years, so that means working in a nursery or working in a preschool or maybe working in a school. But there are such a diverse range of roles out there. I've spent very little time working in a nursery, most of my time has been working for the charity sector, working with other agencies, doing a wide range of roles, but still within early years, and ending up becoming a peripatetic nurture consultant, advisor, trainer and author. I would encourage people to think out of the box. There are so many possibilities.

Jamel There are, and when you map it out and think, like, the standard direction of early years, you would start off by doing an apprenticeship, then go on to be a practitioner, then a room leader, then a third in charge, then a second in charge or deputy manager, area manager and so on, but there's so much more you can do once you have the EY qualifications. You can go on and be SENDCO, you can go on to do occupational therapy and so on, or even Dental Health. The possibilities are endless. But it's about where you see yourself and where best you can apply your key characteristics or your key features of your practice. And where you feel comfortable. I think that's a key thing, where you feel comfortable, because a lot of the time we can be in a place or be sitting in a position and doing a role and we're not actually happy. So that's another important factor.

Sonia   But I think that can change. I think the way you feel comfortable can change, so for example, the job I'm doing now is an emotional job and involves working with really high-level children with social, emotional and mental health needs, often really complex needs. This is my seventh year of doing this particular job. I couldn't have done this job ten years ago. I wasn't in the right space because of the emotional demands with it. But now I'm in a different place, my children are older, now is the right time for me to be doing this job. I just know it, I feel it, I am meant to be doing this now. Three or five years on I may decide I can't do it anymore. Every summer I do question, can I really do another year? And then we get to September, I start the new year and love it again. But, at some point, I will go, no, now is the time to end. It's important to know that what we do now may not be the job we do in five years and that is okay. In all of this we need to be kind to ourselves.

Jamel   Being kind to yourself, knowing where you're at, knowing what seat you're actually sitting in, in the moment, being present. Reflection, reflection, reflection. Being kind to yourself, that is key. Sometimes I'm sitting down and after a long day I'm trying to process all the different things that have happened. Things that I could have done better. Things that I have done well. And thinking, ok, what is the plan of action for the new day? What is the plan of action for the new year, the new term? It is so important that we do that; it gives us a higher level of awareness. So, when you go back in there, you're on the ground or you're in these meetings, you know how best to articulate yourself, how to approach various scenarios and how to equip yourself. And I think also, when we've done all these things, considering all we've just discussed, it helps us then to build better connections with our teams, better relationships with our families. And we're able to create a flow, because we all are the captains of our own ships, but when we're all moving in unison, we're then able to best approach any task that's presented to us.

Sonia   Yeah, absolutely. But I think to be able to do that, for me, underpinning all of that, is back to that being kind to ourselves, really prioritising our wellbeing. I guess for me that's an important way of concluding the book – that we cannot, and I think we probably said this at the beginning, but we cannot support a child's wellbeing, we cannot enable the families that we work with and the children that we work with to have the best possible start if we ourselves are not in a good place. Yes, we absolutely have to prioritise our wellbeing, and that is not a luxury, that is not about spending lots of money and all that kind of stuff, but it is about recognising what makes me feel ok. Recognising when it's all getting too much and when I'm really tired and when I'm really stressed. What are the signals? What's my body telling me? How am I listening to my body? And what am I doing about that? How am I taking care of myself? Am I eating well? Am I drinking well? Am I getting enough sleep? Am I exercising? So, for me, we've joked about it all the way through but it's this, if things are bad, I'm in cold water; if things are good, I'm in cold water; if things are really bad and stressful, I swim in cold water even more, because I know that will reset me, I know that will really help me. I'm not saying everybody should go out and swim in cold water, but it's that whole, find your thing, find out what works for you, what makes you feel ok, that helps you to thrive, not just survive.

Jamel   Yeah, bringing it back to the essence of what brings you joy. When you're feeling down and burdened and tired, giving yourself time to reset.

Sonia   What is it that brings you joy? What helps you to reset?

Jamel   I'm not a swimmer, but I like walking alongside water or cycling and so often I would go on a bike ride and ride up to the Thames Tower Bridge and just stand for hours, just watching the water go back and forth, back and forth, and it brings me peace. It helps me to reflect, it helps me to slow down, helps me to breathe. Sometimes we forget about how important it is to do this – breathe. Take a minute out and just breathe and slow down, because things could be going on so fast around you, things could be going so fast, and you haven't given yourself a minute. You haven't given yourself a second. So that's what helps me; just cycling and being next to the water brings me peace.

I might see you one day, like, look there's Sonia!

Sonia   Oh, it's that mad woman swimming!

Jamel   That's the essence of flow. That's what I get from what both of us have said, being still and just being free. Yeah, just being us – not having to think too deep, not having to worry as such. Just being free. Yeah, finding a place of solace.

Sonia   Yeah, finding a place of solace and being happy and who we are.

Jamel   I think that's the main thing. And then on that you can build relationships and then, in turn, you can build on yourself.

Yeah, I like that. I like that because you got me thinking I feel euphoric right now. Yeah, this is really good as this book is therapeutic. That's one thing I can say, and I hope anyone, actually, I don't hope – I know, anyone that reads it will see it as a form of therapy as well as informative.

Sonia   Yeah. Actually, I really hope what they see from this is the fun we've had. I mean, for me, it's just been a blast. It's great. A good way to do a book as well – the easiest book I've ever been involved in. Yeah. It's been fun, I've really enjoyed it, and I'll miss it. I've really enjoyed meeting up with you and having these conversations, it's been enlightening and enriching and, and it's been fun.

Jamel   Yeah, definitely, I've enjoyed it so much. It's just a blessing to be around your energy, and it's been a blessing to have gained some insight into the way you think, the way someone else thinks, it's really nice. Through this collaboration we have built a positive relationship.

TIME TO REFLECT

- Reflect on your why, what and who: Why have you stayed in the early years? What do you enjoy about working in the sector? Who in your team do you admire for their practice and pedagogy?
- What relationships have you made during your early years journey? How have those relationships shaped your practice?
- How have positive relationships with your class affected your delivery of support, care and nurturing? Have things become easier or more challenging?
- Remember to put your wellbeing first – we cannot care for others effectively if we are not right within ourselves.

- Take a moment to think about your path into early years – think about those who have influenced you and helped you along the way.
- Take a moment to be thankful for the work you have done and those who have helped you along the way.

Index